FROM THE PIT TO PARADISE

A Story of Redemption from a Survivor of Human Trafficking

BERNADETTE KEANE

From the Pit to Paradise

Copyright © 2021, Bernadette Keane.
Contact the Author via e-mail at bernzfree1@gmail.com.

All rights reserved. No part of this book may be reproduced, stored in a retrieved system, or transmitted in any form or any means, electronic, mechanical, photocopying, recording, scanning, or otherwise, without the prior written permission of the author.

Author: Bernadette Keane
Editors: Anjeanette Alexander
Publication Services: Kingdom News Publication Services, LLC.

DISCLAIMER
All the material contained in this book is provided for educational and informational purposes only. No responsibility can be taken for any results or outcomes resulting from the use of this material.

While every attempt has been made to provide information that is both accurate and effective, the author does not assume any responsibility for the accuracy or use/misuse of this information.

Printed in the United States of America.
ISBN 978-1955127035

Introduction

I'm writing this book to try to reach the lost and broken women who may have been victims of human trafficking or addicted to drugs and alcohol. I can tell you that when it came to living a lifestyle of destruction and sin, I was number one at it. It's only by the grace of God that I am alive today to share my testimony. I know that I will have family members reading these words and I want to be very clear that I did not set out to hurt or embarrass anyone. There are things I have written that might make my children uncomfortable, especially my sons. It has not been easy to put these things down in writing. I've shed many tears as these words were written. I've had to face many demons from my past through this process. If you are reading this, just know I did this to help others. God has given me the desire to help single mothers. I know how hard it is to raise kids with little to no help. I also know that the answer to healing and moving forward can only truly be reached with the precious blood of Christ. I am in no way perfect and God is still working on me, but how grateful I am that He was patient with me and gave me so many chances.

I'd like my children to know that I love them very much, and I am sorry for not being the best mother. I want my oldest son, Brian to know that no matter what I have always loved him and regretted not raising him. I know he was better off at the time, but he deserved to be a bigger part of my life. It was my goal to finish this book in 2020 and as I write these final pages, it is New Year's Eve with only a few hours left until 2021. We have been on the island for 5 years. I have come to appreciate everything and everyone in my life. I stopped gripping and started thanking God for the abundant blessings He has poured out in my life. I have forgiven everyone who has hurt me along the way, and I ask for forgiveness for anyone that I may have hurt. I am believing that God will open doors for me this coming year and help me get my ministry started. I have a dream to open up a secondhand store that will benefit single moms who are struggling. I want the Lord to use me to enhance His Kingdom. It does not matter where we start out in our journey; it's where we end up that really matters. I have been literally pulled up from the muck and the mire of a sinful, selfish life. I was absolutely miserable and tried everything wrong to cover the pain. It's not until we totally surrender to Jesus that real healing begins! Thank you, Lord, for bringing me from the pit to paradise!

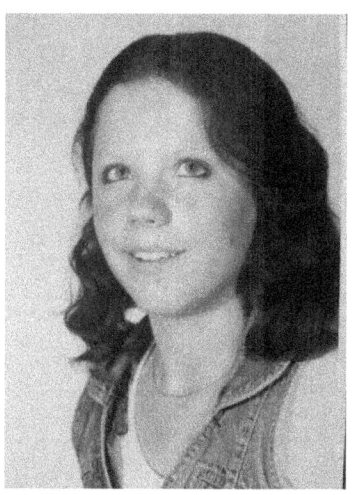

This is the picture my family used on my missing persons flyer when I was taken and introduced into the human trafficking world. As I look at this picture, I see a young innocent girl whose innocents was stolen and led me into a lot of heartache that I didn't have to face. I'm thankful that I finally found peace and purpose in the Lord Jesus Christ.

Table of Contents

Home Life 1

Not My Intent 17

Traveling...26

Home Sick...37

Pregnant Again 58

The Misery Continues 76

Young and Selfish..94

Making Changes 103

The Devil is a Liar 124

More Loss 133

New Beginnings 142

Learning to be Grateful 155

Chapter 1

Home Life

Being born into a large Catholic family, I fell in the middle of eight kids. My parents used the rhythm system, but it didn't work out for them. Five girls and three boys, we lived in a three- bedroom house so that meant we always had to share a room with someone. My earliest memories were of the kindergarten where I attended St. Peter's School in Riverside, New Jersey. Riverside is a small town, one square mile with a bar on almost every corner. I remember the big, yellow bus picking us up to bring us to the school. I had one of the meanest nuns in the school, Sister Severn. I'll never forget the time we were standing for morning prayers and I was too afraid to ask if I could use the restroom. I tried my hardest to hold it, but as I stood in my blue, checkered uniform, the warm urine ran down my legs into my patent leather shoes. My embarrassment must have been apparent as my face began to burn red while the janitor came to the classroom to mop up my mess. My mother was called to bring me a change of underwear.

My next memory of that awful school was Sister Severn slamming her ruler down on the desk so hard it startled me. She was angry that a class full of five-year old's were being noisy and she informed us that our trip to the Philadelphia Zoo was now cancelled. The disappointment was overwhelming. The only other thing that I remember about St. Peter's was the time I was sitting on the bus sneaking a piece of a jelly donut from my coat pocket to my mouth. As I sat there enjoying the treat, one of the nuns on the bus asked me if I was eating something. I quickly lied and said no. That night as I lay in my bed, I thought how I would surely go to hell for lying to a nun. Thankfully, Catholic school was getting much too expensive for my father with so many kids, so the following year I was enrolled at Riverside Elementary School.

The young years were pretty normal. I enjoyed my first-grade teacher, Miss. Hinson. She was kind and soft spoken with patience enough to deal with our class. At home, things were normal. My father worked at the local post office while my mother stayed home to take care of the family. My father enjoyed hunting and fishing with his friends, and they would hang out and drink beer. He seemed to be pretty happy back then. We never did anything together as a family, no vacations or trips down the shore like other people, but I do remember going to an Irish Festival once where we went into a lake in our clothes. I remember the drive home sitting in the back of his truck in soaking wet pants. That was one of the few good times I had with my father as a child.

I guess drinking beers and having a buzz were a great escape for my dad. That was all getting ready to change when he was informed by his doctor to stop drinking alcohol due to a painful bout of gout. After he stopped drinking, it was as if reality hit him in the face. He hated his job at the post office, and he had a house full of kids. It was after that we were to be seen and not heard. I can honestly say he never ate a meal with us. He stopped talking to us all together, and anything that needed to be said was delivered by my mother. When he came home from work, we would scatter like mice to our bedrooms. He didn't even want to see us and spent many hours in his workshop in the basement. Occasionally, he would yell up like a troll under a bridge telling us to pipe down. My poor mother did her best to quiet us. She was a bag of nerves, always worried about getting him mad. She was so dependent on him for everything.

I can still remember the times when my father would be in rare form, and my mother would have us huddled in the bedroom hushing us to keep him from being angry. We would look at her and ask her why she tolerated it and why she allowed him to control her in every way. One time she stood by the door crying saying, "What can I do? He pays for everything, and he had my teeth fixed." Little by little, my anger and hatred grew for my father. As time went on, he became more paranoid of everything. He restricted us from anything fun. We weren't allowed to sleep over anywhere at any time, and we could not use hair dryers or curling irons. There were no school activities or sports because if we got hurt, it would cost him money.

He stopped allowing us to have Christmas, and we sure did miss that silver tree with the spinning colored lights. He shut off the heat in the entire house and had a Franklin stove installed in the living room. It was freezing in the wintertime, and we could blow smoke in our bedrooms. He hated the phone company, but it was a necessary evil. He didn't want us using the phone, so he built a green box, put a lock on the phone, and locked the phone in the box. We used to unscrew the hinges on Tuesday night when they went shopping for groceries. Each of us would make a call to a friend really quick before they came home. We looked forward to shopping night because we got to let loose, make noise, fist fight, and run through the house. With eight kids my mother had to make the food money stretch each week, so snacks were limited. On shopping night, we would sneak spoonfuls of peanut butter and sugar. I remember my mother telling me she had $100 a week for food. We had a steady menu of hotdogs, macaroni and cheese, and other minimal meals with Saturday night being the best with spaghetti and meatballs—at least we got full on that. I'm not saying we weren't provided for. We got fed, and it was always just enough. I would go to my friend's house, and we would raid the refrigerator. I would shove packs of pop tarts in my book bag with other snacks to take home. We were limited to one bath a week, usually on the weekends. He had the hot water shut off to save money, so we had to wait for the water to heat up. My mother would fill the tub with a small amount of water and quickly scrub us down with Ivory soap. She used the soap on our hair as well, and it made it very dry and coarse. I still don't use Ivory soap to this day.

I was about six or seven when I fell down the front steps and skinned the top of my nose. I used to pick at it, and it took a long time to heal. This infuriated my father. I was a fair-skinned Irish girl and would get sunburn on my nose in the summer. I would peel the skin when it bubbled, and my father would get so angry at me. I remember he made me stand in front of him so he could check to see if I had been peeling my nose. "I'm gonna make you my little project," he spewed. I was literally terrified of him and tried to avoid him at all costs. I spent summers being punished in the backyard for picking. I would stand by the locked gate and watch the other kids running and playing up and down the street. Having absolutely no freedom would play a big role in the wicked plans Satan had for me in the future. I guess I was about nine or ten when I brought home good grades. I remember my father telling my mother I think we will have the least trouble out of Bernadette. That statement couldn't have been farthest from the truth. They had already disowned my oldest sister for marrying a black man, but I would be the one to turn my father's hair gray.

As I began to go through puberty, I was getting really tired of the restrictions. All my friends had freedom, and they had nice clothes that were in style. My mother got most of our clothes at the local thrift shop. With eight kids we always had hand-me-downs. My hair was super curly and frizzy from the Ivory soap. It would be an understatement to say I felt like the ugly duckling among my friends. Makeup was out of the question, but we would sneak it at a friend's house. If my father found any of us with makeup, he would confiscate it. He had quite a collection in his workshop. My older siblings began partying, smoking weed and drinking, so my father also had a collection of rolling papers and pot pipes as well. I was eleven when I started hanging out with the "wrong crowd." I met a girl a few streets away named Diane. Diane had a home life completely different from mine. She had one older sister, and she was spoiled to the max. Her room was full of all the things I never had. She had a record player with tons of albums. Her walls were covered with posters of Leif Garret, Dustin Hoffman, The Cars, and other heartthrobs of the late 70's. Unlike me, Diane was allowed to cake on the makeup and blow dry her thick, blond hair. She was allowed to stay out late, while I had to be home by 8:30 before dark. I would go to her house and try to fix up my appearance with her cosmetics. Diane was more advanced than me, so fast and boy crazy. She was high energy and exciting to hang around. It wasn't long before she had me smoking cigarettes in the alley and chasing boys. Her mother used to make trips downtown and always came home with the latest editions of *Teen Beat* and *Tiger Beat* magazines for Diane and new makeup. I was envious of her and hated the way she treated her mom who was fighting cancer. I remember Diane screaming at her mom after a chemo treatment while she was in the tub puking. I thought about how she gets all these things I coveted, and she treats her mom like crap.

The drinking age back then was 18, and Diane looked older. We would get dolled up and go downtown to Bar's Liquor Store, and Diane would purchase quarts of beer. While she kept the elderly man that owned the store occupied, I stole half pints of brandy off the shelf. We would make our way back to the railroad tracks to guzzle beer and brandy and act ridiculous. Once we were done, we walked around Scott Street looking for cute boys. My fun was always short-lived because of my early curfew. Visine and chewing gum were essential to getting away with my secret sins. It wasn't long before my parents caught on to the fact that I had followed in the footsteps of my siblings and began the party life. Nightly exams of checking my eyes and smelling my breath became routine. As the months passed and my anger grew at my lack of freedom, I began to care less and less. I was eleven the first time I smoked pot. I found a joint in the park and smoked it with a good friend, Bobby D. I didn't get high but pretended I did. It took me about seven times before I actually felt the effects of weed. We were back behind the chocolate factory smoking before going to the church carnival at St. Casimir's. Diane and I got on the scrambler, and the weed hit me like a ton of bricks. I was laughing uncontrollably as my comb fell out of my pocket, and I was reaching behind Diane's butt to retrieve it. I had found my new love. Weed became all I wanted, and I did all kinds of shady things to get my hands on it. I became a good thief or so I thought. I would steal from my brother who had a job and kept his money locked in a box in his room. I used the phone box trick unscrewing the hinges and taking loose change and speed pills. We shoplifted from the News Agency store.

Slipping the current issue of *High Times* magazine and Milky Way bars into my pocket was a frequent occurrence. I didn't feel the guilt I had so many years ago when I had lied to the nun. I had attended church every week with my mother. I walked hurriedly every Sunday to sit in the church with Stations of the Cross on the wall and the large, stained glass windows with Saints and Mother Mary looking down on me. I never felt love or acceptance there. We all went through the motions of stand, sit, kneel, pray, use holy water, and genuflect before entering our pew. I had made my first communion and confirmation. I went to confession from time to time at the urging of my mother. I said, "Forgive me, Father for I have sinned." It's been four weeks since my last confession. I always told the same sins—I lied, I disobeyed my parents, blah, blah, blah. We were forced as young teens to attend CCD classes, but we would skip out and eventually just stopped going. We had the little, white church envelopes with the dime inside, and we would take it to Pat's general store and buy candy with it. As I got older and was running around downtown with Diane, I would see the husbands of the women at the church. They would be cruising around checking out us young girls in our tight jeans. The Catholic Church meant absolutely nothing to me. It wasn't till years later I would think about the fact that they had beer gardens at that carnival. It didn't take me long to realize I was not Catholic. I was just forced to go to church.

My party life was all I cared about, and it cost money to

buy beer and weed, so I took my thievery to the next level. My father was having the house painted, and he had $600 lined up twenty-dollar bills in a row behind the TV in his room. I went in on three separate occasions and slipped a twenty from the piles. A lock was placed on my parents' door after that stunt. Diane and I had started going around the neighborhood collecting for MS or UNICEF. We would take the money to party. One day while we were on lunch break walking around town, there was a table outside of Kessler's clothing store that had men's jeans on it. We were laughing and fooling around when I ran up and grabbed a pair of jeans and we all ran to the park. I tossed the pants in a trash can and thought nothing of it. There were four of us: Diane, Ann, Audrey and myself. One day, we all got called down to the office. We had no idea why the cops were there until they asked where the pants were. We were all arrested for theft and taken to the police station. I'll never forget the loud slap on Diane's cheek when her mother came to get her. I was now the bad influence kid that the parents began to dislike. I was on a bad road fast, and it wasn't getting any better the older I got.

My next little scheme would have me paying a higher price. My mother had an old lady friend, Diane, and I knocked on her door collecting for more party money. I, being the thief, asked if I could use the bathroom upstairs while Diane kept her busy. I slipped into her bedroom and opened the jewelry box on her dresser. I grabbed a few rings and we were on our way. I traded the rings to the weed man and didn't give it a second thought.

I was sick of the rules, and Diane and I talked about running away to Philly all the time. The day came when we would put our plans to action. We packed sandwiches and some clothing and headed to the bus stop. I unfortunately told my sister Margaret my plan, and she snitched on me. My heart sunk as my father pulled up in his truck with the bus right behind him. I was taken home and from there was placed in a shelter in Burlington called Crossroads. I loved it there. My parents came for one counseling session, and after two weeks I was sent back home.

I hated being home because nothing changed. I continued to get high and drunk and run around with Diane. I had a little more freedom now because my father didn't want me to run away. I was allowed to stay out till 9:30. Uncle Jimmy, my dad's brother was a Riverside cop. I started seeing my dad's truck parked behind the police station. I knew something was wrong, so I ended up running away again. I stayed at my friend Ann's house for a few days. Ann's mom was the cool mom. She was a barmaid at a local bar called Vince's. She didn't mind that I was there. She was never home anyway. Ann's brother stole money from a guy that was living there, and they blamed me. We got into a fight, and they called the cops on me. I was taken home and was notified that I would be going to court in Mt. Holly that Friday. Those rings I stole had come back to haunt me also. Turns out the weed man took the rings to the Pennsauken Mart to pawn them. When he found out they were antique and worth a lot of money, he acted like a fool and got arrested with the rings and weed. He ratted on me as well as Diane. My dad had also been stealing my roaches of weed and saved up enough to get me charged with possession. They took the door off the hinges to my bedroom and kept me in my bra and underwear until Friday. He had a strip of wood nailed over the window so I couldn't leave. Friday came, and I went to court and was placed in the detention center in Pemberton. I was so scared, but when I got there it wasn't so bad. There was only one other girl in there. There were tons of boys, and most of them were black. I hadn't been around a lot of black people. There were a few black families in Riverside, but these boys were different, they were street smart and I was in puberty. I would sit with the guard and watch these boys play cards. They were nothing like the corny white boys I was used to. They talked game, they had finesse, and I was fascinated by them. If my dad disowned my sister for marrying a black guy, then he just made a mistake putting me in here with these boys. I was charged with grand theft and possession and went back and forth between the detention center and the Jins

Shelter. My father had a good job, but the lawyer fees he was forced to pay were getting expensive. I was eventually released to go home, but things were just heating up for me. I had no intention of staying on the straight and narrow. I continued to party and hang out. I hated my home life, and my next run-away trip would take me further. One day my sister and I made my mom mad, and my dad came home from work and hit us with a stick. My mother was hanging wash in the yard, and we slipped out the front door and headed for the highway. My sister was actually pregnant with her first baby, but my parents didn't know. We hitchhiked down the highway, and she got scared and turned back. I was the crazy one. "I'm not going home," I told her, and I continued to hitchhike down the highway. I didn't know where I was going, but I didn't care either. Anything was better than living in that house; I hated it. I hated my father and I used to ask the devil to kill him. I never felt loved; the fear he instilled in me as a young girl had turned me bitter. He never hugged us or told us he loved us.

He called us sluts when we were still virgins. He told us we were worthless and would amount to nothing. He spoke curses on us, and I had a dark road ahead of me due to the lack of love and affection. I ran to the car that pulled up beside me as my sister faded down the highway to go home. I sunk into the front seat with the stranger and said just take me anywhere. As we headed down Route 130, I was numb, not thinking about the dangers I could face until we reached a sporting goods shop. He had to run inside and as I looked at the advertisement on the wall, I saw guns, fishing tackles etc. I thought this guy could kill me.

I waited in that car anyway, not knowing what would happen. I had been hitchhiking for the past few years with Diane, and I hadn't had any problems. Fear of my father ran deep, but I wasn't scared of thumbing a ride. Thankfully, the guy that picked me up took me to a runaway shelter in Trenton called Anchor House. This place was great, and I loved it there. It was run by a nun named Sister John. She was totally different from the mean Nun of my early years. She didn't wear the black and white uniform, and she was kind and loving. She called my parents and told them I was there. It was a good thing that she was a Catholic nun because my father wasn't in a hurry to force me home again. I had my own room there with a nice, big, comfortable bed all to myself. In the morning, the sun would shine through the pretty curtains as the church bells rang loudly next door. I loved helping to set the table and the food was awesome. I could live here forever, I thought. The basement was set up as a recreational room complete with foosball and a pool table. There were a variety of kids here, boys and girls. More black boys were there, and they were three brothers. They made me laugh all the time. We cracked jokes and shot pool. My parents came up and met Sister John. She talked them into letting me stay for a few weeks.

She took a liking to me. When she found out I had never seen the ocean, she planned a trip for just the two of us. It's amazing how God used a Catholic nun to pour into my life as a young girl. The love she showed me was something new. I remember pulling up to the beach and getting out to walk toward the water. I was amazed at the size of the ocean. Water that just went on and on as far as I could see. I loved it and was very grateful for the gift she gave me. After a few weeks, I was once again sent back home. I would try to be good for a while, but always fell back into my wicked ways. I actually graduated from 8th grade. I remember after graduation my mother told me how I embarrassed her because I had sat the wrong way in the stupid dress I was wearing. Those words cut me to the bone. I was actually thinking about trying to do better and do something with my life. I wanted to go to Votech High School where I could learn a trade. I went to the orientation and chose cosmetology. Diane was going to go with me, but when my father found out, he said that I couldn't go if Diane was going. He lost that battle because neither one of us went. We both started at Riverside High School.

I wasn't really doing much better at school. We were smoking pot every day before class. One day we were in the hallway waiting to go to homeroom when Diane had her eyes closed tightly. She was so high that she smashed her face into the wall. "Open your eyes, Diane," I yelled at her. She snapped out of it and was sent to the nurse. I only made it the first few weeks into my freshman year. Long enough to learn my name was Beatrice in Spanish and long enough to fall asleep in science while sitting at a lab desk. I had stolen Percocet from my friend's mom and passed out in school. Things were so different back then. I don't think I even got in trouble for that stunt. That was the last thing I remember from my short time in 9th grade. Wheels were in motion for the dark chapter that laid ahead. The freedom I had longed for, the feeling of worthlessness, and lack of love had set me up to be led down the dark end of the street.

Chapter 2

Not My Intent

One night after dinner, I was doing the dishes with my sister when we got into a fist fight. She was a year older than me, and we never got along. She had anger and was very mean to me growing up. She got the best of me in the fight, and the last thing I remember before running out of the house was my father laughing at me. I was barefoot when I left. I was supposed to meet Diane downtown, but that wasn't going to happen. My life was about to change.

As I walked towards town with no shoes on, I was still angry at how my father was laughing at me. A car pulled up alongside me, and I recognized the driver. He was a guy that had done a few years in jail for killing Ann's little brother while drinking and driving. He had been riding his big wheel near the bar and was hit. I guess he had just been released. He was ugly and fat. He asked if

I needed a ride downtown and I said yes. He had a friend with him and told me to take a ride with him to Cherry Hill to drop his friend off then he would bring me back. I agreed I figured I would save my feet some hurt. We dropped off his friend, and he told me to hop up front. He was at least 25 and I was 15. It wasn't long before he put his fat hand on my leg. I spit on him and jumped out of his car. I had only been with a few boys. I wasn't very experienced in sex, and this guy made me sick. Here I was on the highway with no shoes, and I had no idea where I was and had no sense of direction.

I had done my share of hitchhiking. I remember making my way down to Florida when I was 13. I had burned my bridges and I tried to get back into the Anchor House, but that was over. Sister John had gone out of her way to get me into a rehab in the Pocono Mountains. I only lasted a few weeks there before getting kicked out. Anchor House had washed their hands of me. I stuck my thumb out on the busy street in Trenton after that rejection. A guy picked me up, and I told him I wanted to go to Florida. I wanted to be near the ocean where it was sunny and warm. This guy had a CB radio, and he called on some truckers to see who was heading south. I ended up with a grimy trucker on my way to Orlando. I had my period and when we stopped at a truck stop, this guy tried rubbing on me and pushed me up against his truck. I cried and told him I had just lost a baby and to please leave me alone. I was bleeding. I have no idea how I came up with that lie. He left me alone, and I ended up in Orlando looking for a laundromat to wash my bloody clothes. The next pervert I met was worse.

He came up to me, and I asked him how far the beach was. He said he would take me there. I finished my laundry and got in his van. He asked me if I liked to drink and offered me some vodka and orange juice. I drank as he drove to the beach. Next thing I remember was waking up in the back of the van, and he was looking at the girls on the beach. He was a pig. I must have been really stupid back then because I went to his house to shower. I was just a kid. My parents had no idea where I was. I was a ward of the state and fled from one of the shelters. This guy had a young, pretty daughter that came home while I was there. I thought what this girl could be thinking that her father has a 13-year-old girl in the house. He wanted to take me to the drive-in movies that night and with nowhere else to go, I agreed. When we got to the drive-in and the movie came up, it was a porno called Flesh Gordon. It was disgusting, and I told him I wanted to leave. I told him to drop me off on the highway that leads to California. He took me to the exit of Highway 1. I jumped out and stuck out my thumb. I was relieved when the first car to pull on the off ramp was a Florida State trooper. I ran up to his car and confessed that I had run away from New Jersey. I had one day of freedom in Orlando before he dropped me off at a detention center. This detention center had a lot of girls. We shared stories and told each other our crimes. There were a few girls in there for prostitution, but I had no idea what they were talking about. I was flown back to New Jersey and locked up there a few weeks before going home again.

Now, here I was again on the highway with no shoes, not sure what direction to go to get back to Riverside. As I stood with my thumb out, I heard a whistle from a small apartment building. I looked over to see two black guys calling me over. I was supposed to be home by 9:30, so maybe these guys would give me a ride.

The enemy had other plans for me that night. It was as if everything that had led up to this night was orchestrated by an evil force. All the chances I took, all the cars I had jumped in and out of over the past few years. My lack of fear, my desire to be loved, the freedom I longed for, the low self-esteem, it had brought me to this moment and I had no idea how much taking the ride from a pervert in Riverside was about to set me on a path of destruction that would completely destroy me for many years to come. As I approached the two guys, they held out a tray of weed and asked me if I smoked. They didn't have to ask twice before I was rolling up a joint. I explained to them I had to be home by 9:30, and they promised to take me home. We sat and talked and after a few minutes two girls came out of the apartment. These girls were dressed nice. They had fancy clothes and makeup. I never saw these kinds of girls before. The guys had diamond rings and big cars. I thought to myself, "Man, these people must be rich."

Time was ticking, and it was getting darker. After everything I had already been through, I still was afraid of my father. I knew I would be in trouble if I was late. I was stoned by now and kept asking them to please get me home on time. We got into the car, and they drove to a local motel. I had no idea what was going to happen, but when they got me into the room, both of them raped me. I was crying and scared. It was way past my curfew, and it was clear these guys were not taking me home. I was kept for several days in that room. I was groomed by these people. They told me I had to choose between them who I wanted to be with. I still didn't understand what they were talking about when they said I would work for one of them. I picked the one that I considered better looking. His name was Slim, and the other one was Prince. The prettier girl was with Slim. Her name was Candy. She had big boobs and a nice body. She was given the task to prepare me for my new profession, the one those girls in the Florida detention center talked about. Candy cut my hair and blew it dry. I was petite, 5ft tall and 100 pounds. They dressed me up in a tight, fancy dress and put makeup on me. My bare feet now had high heels. As I stood and looked into the mirror, I no longer saw the ugly girl with frizzy hair. I saw someone pretty looking back at me. I never thought I had a nice shape, but with the dress I was wearing, I actually looked sexy. I liked it; the transformation was amazing. The attention I felt was when they complimented me was exciting.

In the back of my mind, I thought of my parents. I knew my father was a worry wart. With my past history of running away, I knew that they thought that is what I did. I had no intention of running away that night. I wanted nothing more than to have them drive me home, but now it was too late. It had been five days now and Bernadette was gone. I was told to choose a new name, and Slim had real identification made for me. I picked the name Crystal and that's who I became. I was schooled on what was expected of me with my new job. I was a quick study and a good student. I was told what to say if I was arrested. I had to memorize my new birthdate and I even had a social security card. I was told, if questioned by the police to stick to my story and don't tell them how old I really was or my real name. I was told I would be meeting men and making money. I was taken to the Cherry Hill Mall to get a wardrobe for myself. I remember seeing several girls there from my school. I don't think they would have recognized me now. I wondered what was going on at home. No matter what my father had done to me and his lack of love and affection, I was riddled with guilt knowing he was worried about me. I figured he was blaming himself for laughing at me as I ran out the door the week before. I had to push the guilt and those thoughts of home to the back of my mind. I was Crystal now, and this was my new life.

Once they thought I was ready, I was sent out to Federal Ave. in Camden. I was so close to home, but so far away. During the first few days, Candy worked with me. I was taught how to use a condom without the date knowing. I was told what to charge and not to take less. This was the early 80s, and things were completely different on the streets than they are now. There were rules to this game, and not following the rules could get you hurt. Most, if not all, the girls out there had a pimp. It was dangerous not to have a man looking out for you. They convinced us they had our best interests by having us selling our bodies and giving them the money. We were given a certain amount for clothes, and we had our own motel rooms to work out of. I won't lie; in the beginning, it was fun and exciting. I had this sense of freedom while being enslaved in sex trafficking. No more curfew, no more ugly duckling. I had a key to my own room. I was making so much money as the new, young girl out there. If I wanted new clothes, I got them. I learned how to do my own hair and makeup. I remember sitting in the back seat of the Cadillac heading toward the city lights at night. We would snort coke off Slim's pinky nail to keep us upbeat and on our toes. There weren't a bunch of crack heads out there back then. Yeah, we snorted a little coke and smoked weed, but we dressed nice, kept ourselves clean, and always used condoms. There were other rules, too.

The pimps that got a hold of me were from Baltimore. They had Maryland tags on the car. They traveled in a group. Once you picked one to be with, you weren't allowed to talk to any other pimp. If you were working on the streets and a pimp approached you, the rule was that you completely ignored them and turned the other way. You couldn't even look at them. If you were weak and talked to another pimp, they had the right to tell you to break yourself. That meant you had to give that pimp any money you had on you. Then you had to face your pimp and endure the punishment. I never got into trouble with any other pimp. I was content with Slim and Candy for a while. I was focused and determined to learn the streets, and I did just that. Every once in a while, the cops did a sweep to clear the streets and see who the new young girls were. I was arrested one night and taken to the Camden County Jail. Here I was 15 with a fake ID. The cops knew I was young. They pressed me for my real name and age, but I would not crack. I passed the test and spent a week in the adult jail. It was horrible;

the women in there were old and haggard. Most of them were heroin addicts that asked for my sugar packets. There were killers in this jail unlike the detention center I was used to. I was given a bail and court date, and Slim was there to pick me up on my release. I was proud of myself when I got into the car, and he praised me for passing the test of being locked up and holding my own. The court date for me would never come because Camden was getting hot, and the cops were on to this group of outsiders from Maryland that had young girls working on their streets. Pimping could get these guys a lot of time in jail, so they had to stay a step ahead of the law. Candy was starting to get on my nerves because she was getting jealous of the praise I got from Slim. I was making more money than her, and she was bossy. I wasn't the weak girl crying in the motel room like I had been the night they set the trap for me. I was getting street smart and wanted to do it my way. I didn't need her to school me anymore. She was trying to get me in trouble with Slim by telling him I was refusing to do certain things. It was true; several times when we worked together I refused to do things I was not comfortable with. I felt like it was my choice at that point, and the money I was making was good enough. Even I had a limit of what I would be forced to do. I was strong-willed, and she didn't like it. Next stop was Atlantic City.

Chapter 3

Traveling

Atlantic City was a completely different beast! I had no idea this place existed in New Jersey. The casinos and the fast-paced action were intoxicating to me. This place was full of perverts who spent big money.

Atlantic Ave. was the strip there. I had been working more on my own there because my relationship with Candy was rocky. There was a girl who I met named Tennessee. She was a tall redhead that didn't take crap from anyone. We went on a few double dates, and I saw her in action one night when a couple of young guys tried to take advantage of us. She set them straight and we got away from them. I liked her and looked for her every night. We got along great. In the daytime I would go down to the beach. I saw this guy walking a little dog up and down the beach. I had a feeling that he was in the game because he had a lot of gold jewelry. Unlike Slim who dressed in suits and wingtip shoes, this guy was more laid back in a jogging suit and sneakers. Slim was starting to be strict, and I was getting fed up with his rules. We had to say yes instead of yeah. He didn't want us to wear jeans unless they were dry cleaned with a pleat going down the front. It was getting on my nerves between the way Candy was treating me and all his stupid rules. Come to find out the guy I had been checking out on the beach was a pimp and his girl was Tennessee. I was ready to make a move and break myself. I didn't know what trouble this was going to cause for me down the line, but I did it. I chose to be with pimp number two and his name was Ricco with his little dog, Chicco. He had 3 girls, Tennessee, Carol, and a black girl named Cherry. Ricco liked me right away and was excited to add me to his stable. Slim was not so happy to be losing a good money maker, but that was the way the game was played, so I joined my new family. I had been taken in September around the third week. I was in Camden for about a month and after a few more arrests in Atlantic City, it was time to head south. Ricco and his crew were also from Maryland; they all knew each other and traveled together. When we pulled into a new place, we all got rooms at the same motel.

Traveling to Ft. Lauderdale with my new family was an adventure for me. My short one-day trip a few years earlier reminded me of the warm breezes and palm trees.

Something about the tropical weather attracted me. Ricco had a baby with the girl, Carol. She was kind of dumpy and wasn't as sharp. The baby was in Maryland with his mom. Cherry, the black girl, used to wear wigs and she reminded me of Donna Summers. Tennessee was tall and wasn't really that attractive, so I was feeling like the beauty in this bunch. I was small and short, and Ricco had a soft spot for me. I reminded him of the first girl that turned him onto the life of pimping. Her name was Sugar and he talked about her all the time. In a sick way, I started having feelings for Ricco right away. I loved the attention he gave me, and he treated me good.

All he ever played was Stevie Wonder on the tape player. I learned every word to every song on the *Hotter Than July* album. The trip to Ft. Lauderdale was going great until we ended up stopping at a truck stop in South Carolina. We had to stop and make money along the way for gas and food. Ricco parked the car and was letting the dog run around on the grass, while Tennessee and I hit the lot to make money. Carol and Cherry were traveling in another car and planned to meet us in Florida. Tennessee was a thief, a real thief. When we were in Atlantic City, she took me to the mall and showed me how to boost. She took a giant bag off a rack and stuffed it with all kinds of stuff. She was good at stealing, and that was on her agenda that night at the truck stop.

I was instructed to wait until she was in the back of the truck with the trucker. She would put his pants on the front seat, and I was to climb up and get the money out of his wallet and put it back in his pocket. Everything was going according to plan until I dropped the wallet between the seat and the door. I had gotten the money, but that mistake would cost us. Tennessee got out and we were walking back to Ricco when we saw a cop asking him questions. The cops let him go and set his attention to us. We acted like we didn't know Ricco, and he grabbed the dog and took off. He had one of the very first cell phones. It was giant. We knew how to catch up with him later. The cop questioned us, and he told us to get in the car and he was going to drop us off at the county line. Sitting in the back of his car, I gave the money roll from the trucker to Tennessee. She took it and shoved it down her pants and inside her. I know it's disgusting, but that is what she did. We were almost ready to be on our way when the radio went off in the cop car. A trucker had been robbed by a couple of girls at the truck stop. The cop turned around and started asking us where the money was. We just kept denying it, and we were taken to the local jail. This place was like something out of a movie. It was a little backwoods station that had a few small cells.

They knew we had the money and kept asking us to take them to it. They thought we hid it back at that truck stop somewhere. They searched us both and found nothing. We were booked into the jail, and they kept us a few days. About the third day, a couple of bail bondsmen came to the jail. These were two black guys that were shady. They took our pictures and posted our bail. They knew we had the money, and they wanted to get it. While we were locked up, Tennessee took the money out, washed it off, and we hung up a sheet from the bunk to give us privacy. She counted out twenty-four hundred dollars. This was big money back then. She put the money away again and we waited. So, these crooked bail bondsmen had nothing but evil intentions for us. They told us that they were putting us up in a motel, and we would be working in the club they owned to pay them back for the bail money. We were warned not to pull a fast one because they had our photos and would hunt us down. The whole thing was odd. I don't know if the cops were involved in the club thing and just let them take female prisoners, but the whole ordeal was strange. They put us in a ragtag room and told us we were being watched. The second night in the room they took us out to a club. It was an all-black club, and we were the only two white girls in there.

They kept asking us where the money was. They must have known how much it was because they wanted it bad. We just kept denying it and were waiting to make a getaway. The third night they said we were going to a fair, and someone would be watching us. They even gave us tickets to get on the rides.

We saw the guy they had tailing us. We went on the Ferris wheel and when we got off, we lost our tail and took off. Outside the gates of the fair, we flagged down a cab and asked him to take us to the Georgia state line. He told us it would be $100, and Tennessee took out the money and we were gone. It felt like a weird dream to me. I wasn't worried about the bail bondsmen because they had our fake names of people who didn't really exist. The cab dropped us off in the beginning of Georgia and we were on our way. We started thumbing it and as the sun was coming up, a car stopped and picked us up. It was a couple of Jamaican guys with long dreads and good weed. We sat in the back and got stoned. We were happy to be on our way to Ricco with a pocket full of money. As we drove on our way into the Sunshine State, Tennessee just couldn't help herself. She went into one of the bags in the back seat and stole a camera. I was high and paranoid. This chick was bad news, and she was going to get me hurt.

We survived that ride and eventually made it back to Ricco in Fort Lauderdale. I loved it there, the warm weather and the swimming pools at the motels. Ricco was happy with the big wad of hundreds we handed him. We began to work another Federal Highway there.

One night, I was standing talking to Carol when she said to me, "Here comes that girl." I turned around, and Candy was right on top of me and slams me in the head with a two by four. I immediately saw stars as I was pushed to the ground. I remember her being over top of me and I was kicking her as hard as I could in the chest. Apparently, Slim hadn't taken me leaving him very well and it was payback time. This attack was against the rules. He and Ricco had to work it out. Up until this point, I wasn't experiencing a lot of fear, but Florida had a lot of crazy guys from everywhere. We were warned about not dating guys that were too young. They were usually trouble and didn't feel like they had to pay for it. I made the mistake of getting into the car with a younger guy. It was the first time I had trouble with a date. He tried to keep me in the car, but I escaped somehow. Things were starting to get sketchy, and I was feeling new emotions. Real fear. It didn't stop me, I continued on the wicked path before me. Broward County sheriffs were different from the cops I had dealt with in New Jersey. They had less patience and when they saw a new face on the street, they chased me aggressively and my charges began to multiply. After several arrests of all of us, it was getting too hot and it was time to move on again. They decided we would travel to Hollywood and stop at the truck stops along the way so we could make money. We stopped in different states along the way and hit the strips in Texas and Arizona.

While we were in Texas, the local police made it real clear we were not welcome in that neck of the woods. They were very racist and warned us to depart or the guys would be facing jail time. They knew what was up when they stopped a car with a black guy with tons of gold, driving white girls around in a Cadillac.

It was around November when we finally made it to California. It was a long ride, and it wasn't so fun for me anymore. The very first truck I got into in L.A. was a psycho that tried to restrain me and not let me go. God must have been watching out for me because again I managed to get out. I didn't like this anymore and it showed. I began fighting with Ricco and Tennessee. I started slacking and going in early without making the money he expected. I was fearful in California. It was by far the most dangerous place I had been. You could literally feel the evil hanging over the city. We would be down on Hollywood Boulevard, and there were so many girls and unlike the other places, there were male prostitutes out there as well. I remember the young, flamboyant guys in tight jean shorts. That was strange to me at first, but this place was beyond wicked.

One night, I went to an alley with a Mexican guy. It was a slow night and instead of going with my gut instinct, I got into the car. He drove me away from the strip and the further we drove, the more nervous I became. We pulled into a dark alley and when he realized I had slipped a condom on him, he was furious. He pulled out a small gun and loaded it with bullets from his shirt pocket. He told me to take my dress off and as he loaded the gun, he said, "I'll kill you." I was so terrified that I couldn't shed a tear if I tried. I pleaded with him by telling him I had a young son. He told me to shut up as he went through my small purse. He stole my money and Polaroid pic of me that was in the purse. He was unable to perform and for whatever reason, he threw my dress on me and told me to get out. He said, "If you turn around and look back at me, I'll kill you," he said, "I've killed a hundred girls." I was in shock as I exited the car fumbling with my dress. I quickly made my way down the alley and tried to figure out where I was.

When I arrived back at the motel and informed Ricco what happened, he really didn't seem to care. It was at that moment I began to realize that this guy cared absolutely nothing about me. He wasn't glad I survived the attack, but he was angry that I was broke. I hated being in California, after that happened to me, I was in constant fear. I would pray to get arrested, so I wouldn't have to be out there. We eventually left California.

This time I wasn't able to drive with them. They put me on a plane to Vegas. I remember it was a very short flight. Vegas was another wicked place. They didn't call it Sin

City for nothing. There was a ton of money to make, and hanging out in the casino looking for dates was a nightly ritual. I was fascinated by this place that never shut down. In the early 80s it was less geared toward families and more toward lost souls looking for anything and everything to feed the lust of the flesh. At this point, I wasn't getting along with Tennessee anymore. I did the bare minimum to keep Ricco off my back.

One night, I was sitting in a casino that had big screens for computer gambling. I met a guy that wanted to date me, but he had other guys surrounding him. He told me he wanted to help me get off the street. He said his name was Antonio Brenner. He told me he was Yul Brenner's brother. I gave him my phone number before we headed to a local hotel. He was going to call me and help me get away from Ricco. As we approached the motel, a black guy came out of nowhere and pulled a gun on him. He had a purple crown royal bag full of money, and the guy robbed him. I was scared and took off. The next day, I got a phone call saying, "You better get out of town. You set Antonio up to be robbed." I pleaded with the angry voice on the phone and said, "Why would I give him my phone number if I was going to set him up?" I guess they believed me because nothing happened. I don't know if he was really related to Yul Brenner. I tried to research it and came up empty. Funny thing is he was tall and bald and had bodyguards in the casino and had a foreign accent. I had no idea who Yul Brenner was back then, but it could have very well been him. Nevertheless, my chances of getting off the streets with his help was now ruined. We stayed in Vegas for about six weeks before heading back to Florida. I was tired. It had been a whirlwind the past four months, and I was homesick. I had become a shell of a person with no worth again. If my self-esteem was low before, now it was almost nonexistent. I was heavily drinking every day. Hennessy and Coke was my choice. I was drowning in alcohol to stop the pain.

We finally made it back to Ft. Lauderdale, and I was given my own room due to the fact I was at war with Tennessee. I was sick; my body was tired and weak, and Ricco barely paid attention to me anymore. I was refusing to go out and became a burden to him. I was being pushed around and battered by him, but I didn't care. I had a guy that felt sorry for me and used to give me a couple hundred bucks to keep Ricco off my back. I would just drink and lay out by the pool. Ricco tolerated me for a while, and I told him I wanted to contact my parents. I knew they must have been worried sick about me, and the guilt was eating me up inside. My friend told me he would help me get home if I wanted to leave. As I laid in that Econo Lodge on Federal Highway, it took everything I had to muster up the courage to call my parents.

Chapter 4

Home Sick

I was physically run down and emotionally stripped. Everything about me changed; the way I looked, the way I spoke, and my wardrobe which consisted of tight shiny pants from Frederick's of Hollywood, a fur coat, and snakeskin boots. I was an official hooker. As I dialed my parents' number, I was shaking with fear. It was February and I had been gone since September, seven months of them worrying about me. What am I going to say to them? My mother answered the phone and was shocked to hear it was me. She yelled for my father. I tried to tell her what I had been doing, but she cut me off and didn't want to hear it. "Just come home," she cried, "We've been worried sick about you." The next morning, I was laying in the sun and decided it was time to go home. So, I flew home to New Jersey late that afternoon. I was no longer the same girl that left, and I only had my street walking clothes.

When I first saw my father, I was shocked to see how much he had aged in seven months. He had lost weight and his hair was much greyer. He hugged me for the first time in my life. They begged me not to leave again. I was not ready to go to the house with them, so I asked them to take me to a motel. They checked me into the Garden State Motel in Cinnaminson. They asked if I needed anything and took me to the store for supplies. I was wearing my boots and my fur coat. I was not the girl they remembered. I came back to Jersey a very damaged, young girl.

This experience and the things these men did to me had destroyed me completely. I felt that any bit of good I may have been also destroyed. I was now an actress in my own life, playing a part I was never prepared for. It was a bad movie, a very bad movie, with so many of the characters in pain: myself, my parents, and others. I spoke as if I grew up in an urban city. I didn't even know who I was. I stayed in the motel for about a week before I went back home. My father had a small room built in the basement and I was given my own key to come and go as I pleased. I had no intention of going back to school. I felt like I was a stranger in Riverside. It was boring and slow paced. I was so used to the nightlife and the excitement of the city. It was hard for me to adjust back to the small-town way of life.

I battled with conflicting thoughts because in a sick and twisted way, I loved Ricco. I came to question my feelings towards him and even decided in my mind that it was hard leaving him. I ran around town in my spandex pants and spewed vile language to the cars that slowed down to look at me. I managed to meet one of the few black guys in town named George. We started dating. I asked him if he knew what the game was, and he didn't. I had it in my head that all black guys would know about street life.

My world was completely turned around, and I was absolutely out of control. I was running around drinking and acting like an idiot. Ricco had been calling my house, and it was only a matter of time before I would make my way back to him. It was May when I decided I couldn't stay in Riverside anymore. I decided to meet Ricco in Jersey City. Just like that, I was back in the life. We were set up outside New York and would go to the city at night to work. Ricco had picked up another girl somewhere along the way; her name was Star. Since I no longer got along with Tennessee, I wound up rooming and hanging with Star.

New York was absolutely insane. We worked on 42nd Street with hundreds of other girls. The streets were bustling with every degenerate you could imagine. The girls were almost naked. I myself used to wear a tube top as a skirt. Competition was brutal, and we pulled out all the stops to make money. There was a bus station across from where we worked and when the cops would come, we would all run and hide behind the buses. One night during a sweep, I tried to run, and an undercover cop tackled me to the ground and took me to the station. It was like 2 a.m. and they knew I wasn't 18. They pressured me to give my age and identity. I had the nerve to call my mom in the middle of the night and told her to tell the officer I was 18. She hung up, and I was taken to Rikers Island.

This was a horrific place to be. Killers, addicts, and the worst of the worst. After a week, I was released to a halfway house for underage kids. They found out who I was and were going to send me back home. There was a driver, who had the job to take me to Grand Central Terminal and get me on a bus home. I used my persuasion to convince him to get me a bag of weed and drop me off. I told him I would not stay home, so what was the point. He dropped me off, and I walked down the street smoking a joint and looking at the sea of faces passing me by. Everyone was in a hurry, looking stressed and angry.

Finally, I made my way back to Jersey City, but now Ricco was treating me bad again. I started making plans with Star to leave him. I had become skilled at manipulating people to do what I wanted.

There was a shopping area in Jersey City called Journal Square. I would go there to the little Asian shops where hundreds of cute dresses hung on racks. I thought how much of a good deal it was to buy these dresses for $10 each. I had to replenish my clothing before taking off to the next vile adventure that laid ahead. Star and I took off in a cab one night and headed back to the outskirts of Atlantic City. I knew the area and there was a strip of motels about 20 miles from the city. We stayed there for a few weeks taking cabs back and forth, but the pimps knew we were without protection, so our next plan was to go to Detroit where Star was from.

It's unreal how each city seemed to have its own level of spiritual darkness above it. Detroit had plans for me that would once again change my life forever. We arrived in Detroit and went to a house where a friend of Star lived. This guy was a drug dealer and user. He had dilaudid, which is a narcotic to manage pain. This night was the first time I let someone stick a needle in my arm. I liked the relaxing feeling, but not the throwing up. The side effects made me realize that this was something I was not interested in continuing.

There was a celebration at the Renaissance Center in downtown Detroit. They had just completed construction on two towers. Star and I made our way down there. I remember standing there when a young, black guy came up to me and asked me for money. I told him no, so he punched me in the face. There was a cop standing right there, and I asked him if was going to do anything about it, and the officer just looked at me. I knew this was another evil place, and that nothing good could come from being here.

It didn't take long for us to get picked up by a pimp. This was the final pimp I would ever be with. As the car slowed down, the guy driving offered us a ride. We already knew what was up. He took Star to a friend of his, and I stayed with him. The first thing he did was take me to the local booster, a lady who dealt in stolen clothes. He had me pick out what I wanted, and he took me to an apartment called South Field Towers. It was a nice building with an elevator and a guard in the lobby. It had a nice, big swimming pool and he had a girl named Bonnie living there. At first, she wasn't too happy to share her place with me, but he had to make sure I was going to stick around before getting me my own place. Bonnie and I became fast friends. She liked to snort coke and we would stay up all night talking. I didn't have to work on the streets, either. She had a steady clientele that came to us. These were powerful men: lawyers and judges. I was comfortable there. I laid out in the sun every day and got tanned. I just swam and worked when she set up the dates.

Casper was the name of this hustler, I mean, pimp. When work was slow, he took us to a bar that had a motel attached to it. If you wanted to work there, they had a rule that you had to keep a drink in front of you. One day I was there and being the new face, I was making most of the money. Some of the girls were getting angry, and I had a feeling they were going to try to hurt me. I always carried a straight razor with me for protection. I had been drinking all day, and I was drunk. The barmaid offered me a drink, and I refused because I had enough and I was trying to keep my eyes on the girls. The owner was a short Italian guy named Tom. He kicked me out and as I was leaving going down the steps, he came behind me and started pushing me. I had the razor in my hand and without thinking, I swung at him. I got to the bottom of the steps, and I heard him yelling that B cut me. He came running back down the steps, and he had blood all over his shirt. I had cut him from his nose to his chin and found out later that he needed 13 stitches. He put a contract out on my life because he wanted me dead. Casper took me to a high-end hair salon and had them dye my hair blond. He moved me into my own place away from the towers.

I turned 16 in Detroit. Bonnie and I went to the hair salon to get our hair done, and she told the guy doing my hair it was my birthday. Before we left, he handed me a small vile full of coke. I got along pretty good with Bonnie, but since the hit was out on me, I stayed at my place a lot. There were times where I was forced to go out and work on the streets, but I always felt like I was looking over my shoulder.

Detroit was just as crazy as everywhere else and I realized that I hated the streets. I got locked up a few times and it was starting to get cold. I hated the cold. Things began to go downhill because once again, I didn't want to be out there. I started feeling sick to my stomach a lot and I was craving egg nog. I would buy a big can of it and drink it down then puke. I soon found out I was pregnant. I had always used condoms except for with Casper, so I knew it was most likely his. I walked in my place one day and found him there doing coke with a dancer. I was mad and caused a fuss and told him I thought I was pregnant. He slapped me in my ear so hard that I fell in the tub. I packed up shortly after that and left. I hung around with some more shady characters before realizing it was time for me to go. I hitchhiked to a truck stop and caught a ride back to Jersey. My parents took me back, but not for long. I ended up back in the Jins Shelter. I was a complete mess, and now I was pregnant.

One day, another girl and I ran away from the shelter and

we were hitchhiking down the shore. We got caught in Ocean County, and they put in detention there. I remember how nice it was and the food was great. While there, a group of ladies came to visit the girls and tell them about Jesus. I had been through so much that I was very open to hearing about a savior who loved me and died to set me free. I prayed with those women and asked Christ to come into my heart. I had a peaceful feeling that I never had before. I knew deep down that it was true, and it was real. When the woman called my father to tell him the good news, he was furious. I could hear him yelling at her telling her that I was Catholic and not part of the cult they were in. I was shattered. I didn't understand why he had thought it would be a bad thing for me to live for God. The peace I had that day was short-lived. We were transported back to Burlington County, and I went back to my old ways fast.

Nobody was there to tell me how to stay on the right track with God. I wasn't told how to fight the devil or that I needed to read the bible to fight temptation. I was starting to get along in the pregnancy, and here I was stuck in the shelter. I was told about a maternity home in Trenton for unwed mothers. I agreed to go there, and it was really nice. It was a big older house with a long driveway. It was cozy and comfortable, and I had a nice room. Different volunteers would come and teach us how to crochet and knit. I learned how to make granny squares and began working on a baby blanket. I had no idea what I was going to do with a baby, but I wanted to keep him. I had nothing else good in my life and figured I could love him, and he could love me.

There was a couple that would come to the house, and they were also Christians. I was blessed when they took a liking to me and took me out to buy maternity clothes. They showed me the love of Christ and even took me to Philly to see a live show called Oklahoma. Lori and Mike were their names, and they would visit me every few weeks. There was another lady who was the cook there; her name was Miss. B. She also liked me and treated me well.

These people showed me the genuine love of God when I was at my lowest point in my life and made a big impact on my life. I've never forgotten about them over the years. It's true that someone can plant a seed into your life, and you never realize how much it means to you later in life. I'm grateful God put those people in my path during a time when I was so broken and lost. Just a little bit of love here and there kept me going and would give me a glimmer of hope that I was loved by someone.

There were at least 10 girls in the house, and I was content being there. It was easy to catch the bus to town to shop. There was a park close by that had a bear in a cage. Trenton was a city, so I still had an exciting place to go out when I was bored even if it was just to buy hair supplies. I was in my 8thmonth, and there was one girl who did not like me. She stole something from another girl and put it in my room. I was so angry that I went after her and wanted to fight her. That ruined it for me. I was kicked out the next day. I was there by a court order so that meant back to shelter for me. The court system had enough of my crap, and they forced my parents to take me home. I pretty much cooled my jets after that because I was ready to give birth in a month. I just laid around and waited. I remember my dad asking me if my baby was going to be black. I told him that it was a strong possibility. My mom used to walk to Cumberland Farms a few times a week for milk and bread, and she would get me a can of ravioli and a Milky Way bar. When I had trouble sleeping, she would fix me warm milk, and it always seemed to work. My due date was May 7th, but due to complications I was scheduled for a Cesarean section on Friday the 13th.

I thought it would be easy not going into labor but had no idea what a C section really consisted of. It was a painful, rude awakening when I came out of the operating room. I had 13 staples. It was horrible. I was in there drugged up for like three days and still hadn't seen my baby. My mother was there with my sister, and they had a weird look. I knew something was wrong, and they finally told me my son had swallowed some poop and was sick. I kept thinking there was no way I would be able to take him home. I couldn't imagine myself a mother, and my dad was so paranoid he insisted a priest come to baptize the baby just in case. I still don't understand why the Catholic people think God sends babies to hell if they aren't baptized. Turned out he got better. I named him Brian James, and he was my pride and joy. He was born May 13th, 1983. I turned 17 three months later in August. My mom helped me a lot. I had my room in the basement with my baby, and he was a good boy. I laid him on my chest and sang him songs. I was having a hard time with the staples because they wouldn't heal, and I ended up with an infection. As soon as I recovered from the trauma of surgery and was able to walk, I wanted to go out. I would take him out with me, but a lot of times my mom would watch him.

Being home allowed me to reconnect with old friends. I was back hanging around with Diane and Ann, and we had new habits now that we started snorting lines of meth. Meth was an evil drug that kept us up for days. I started leaving Brian with my mom a lot while I went out to party and do drugs. I just had no social skills or no idea how to be a good mother. I was young and selfish. One night my sister was supposed to babysit Brian at her house, and I was going to go out but decided to go spend time with Brian at my sister's house. When I got there, she told me my parents wouldn't let her take him. I was angry, but after I calmed down. I decided to try to get my life together. There was a small company that sold magazine subscriptions over the phone. I was going to go and apply for the job the next day. I was still 17 and under my parents' roof, so I figured I would try. The next day I went home, and Brian was in the playpen. I went to get him, and my father stormed toward me telling me not to touch him. He grabbed me and started hitting me. He yelled for my mother to grab the scissors he was going to cut my hair. This isn't the first time he would have cut my hair. A few years earlier I had come home one night after a neighbor told my dad I stole $6 from her purse. I did take it. I was drinking and had a hickey on my neck. He had my mom hold me down and he chopped my hair off. It was the most devastating thing that ever happened to me when I was 13. This time I fought back, that was not happening again.

I took off my high heel and hit him in the face with it. I knocked off his glasses. He relented and ended up calling the cops on me. I couldn't believe he was doing this. I came home calm, getting ready to tell them I'm going to get a job. When the cops came, I was informed that I couldn't take my baby anywhere until I was 18. I stuck to my plan and was hired to sell magazines. I was good at it. I was a real hustler and made pretty good money there for the few months they were in town. For all I knew it was a scam. We promised each customer a free 35 mm camera with every purchase. I would get paid, and on the weekends, I would hitchhike to the Pennsauken Mart. I had my older sisters ID and would go to the bar there called Crazy Eddie's, a biker bar. I would drink beer and play centipede on the game machines.

One day while thumbing it down the highway, a cute, blond hair guy picked me up; he had ice blue eyes. We hit it off right away and became inseparable. His name was Dave and I fell head over heels for him. He lived over top of a greasy spoon joint in Riverside called the Palace. There were rooms for rent up there, and that's where I started spending my time. My mother was still taking care of Brian most of the time, and Dave and I were doing drugs together. By this time, I was injecting meth.

On the day I turned 18, I took my baby and moved out with him into Dave's place. I can still see my mother standing at the front door crying and telling me to be careful with him. I was so shot out and selfish. I loved my baby and had everything he needed, but with the drug use, it was just too much for me to care for him. I ended up meeting my parents at a lawyer's office and signing over temporary custody to them. I wanted him safe, and

I knew he would be taken care of with them. He was a beautiful mixed, little boy with big brown eyes, and it killed me to let him go, but I had no life skills at all. I was suffering from the trauma of being a victim of human trafficking, and the only thing that killed the pain was drugs and alcohol. Sometimes I would think of the peace I felt years earlier when I asked Jesus in my heart. It was always in my mind that one day I would get my life right with God. I wanted that peaceful feeling again.

My relationship with Dave was as dysfunctional as everything else in my life. He had a nice car, a Dodge Dart, eventually he lost the place over the Palace, and we would hustle to get motel rooms. Meth addicts are sneaky, lying, and big-time thieves. We used to go to different churches and say we were married and homeless, and they would put us up in a room for a night or two. Sometimes they gave us cash. There were times when we would go to the churches or meetings when programs were taking place, and I would distract members while Dave went on the hunt for the ladies' purses. There was no level of debauchery I would not stoop to in order to get my drugs. As survival became harder, Dave and I began to fight. He was abusive and hit me a lot. I didn't care. I was already used to being abused and treated like crap, so this just went along with the sinful lifestyle I was living.

It was probably less than a year after many trials and tribulations that Dave made the decision to leave me. He had a sister that didn't like me, and she offered to pay his way to Florida to get him away from me. I was left shattered with nowhere to go in the middle of a bitter, cold winter. It wasn't as if I didn't deserve heartbreak and devastation with all the wrong I had been doing to others. It's no lie when they say you reap what you sow. When living life with no other purpose but to feed the lust of the flesh, you can expect emptiness and darkness to be your closest friends.

I wound up going back home with wounded pride. Being back with my son was the only joy I had at that point. I had to get a job if I wanted to stay there in the basement room with my son. I applied at a clothing company a few blocks away called Century Mills. They made socks, underwear, and bathing suits. I was hired to work in the printing room with the printer who made all the tags for the clothing. I was replacing a guy who was a slacker, and there were a bunch of pallets full of boxes of tags that needed to be cut and shipped. I ran a big cutting machine, and again I was great at my job. I liked working because it gave me a sense of worth. I enjoyed accomplishing my task. I got caught up on all the back work, and my three-month review was coming where I would be eligible for company health insurance. I was called to the office and let go. They didn't want to pay for me to have insurance. I had served my purpose and they no longer needed me. I was devastated and cried on the walk home with my box of belongings under my arm. My mother tried to console me by calling the owner a creep. They were Jewish owners, and my father had his own thoughts on the Jews. I remember one time he shaved his mustache like Hitler and came out of his room with a walking stick saying, "Hi Hitler." I didn't know what that meant or who Hitler was, so I didn't know what was supposed to be funny about that.

My father was a strange bird; he did a lot of weird things. He used to go fishing and bring home giant snapping turtles. He would decapitate them and hang them over a bucket from the clothesline. When the blood was done dripping, he would empty the shell and fill it with cement. One time he brought home a big turkey and took it to the basement and chopped off its head. Our family dog, Shannon chased it around with no head. Blood was squirting all over the walls, and it was horrible. He had been a hunter for years, and we had stuffed animals all over the house. Big deer heads lined the walls along with pheasants that looked like they were still in flight. He even had a stuffed squirrel. He had hunter's guilt years later and stopped killing and stuffing animals.

So, here I was with no job and time on my hands again, and you know what they say about idle hands. I was still doing drugs, but working had given me some structure. It wasn't long before I was staying out all night again hanging out with the older crowd that everyone called crankster gangsters. There was an older guy, Mike, that I was attracted to and although I still was broken-hearted, I ended up hooking up with him one night. He left me stranded the next morning when he said he was going to get donuts. He made sure to take my ring off the side of the tub before he left. It was a month later when I felt that familiar feeling of needing to puke after eating. One morning, after running to the bathroom while eating a bowl of raisin bran, I had to break the news to my mother that I thought I was pregnant again. This was just great. I already lost custody of my firstborn due to my selfish ways, and here I am carrying baby number two.

The next time I saw Mike, I hit him in the face for stealing my ring. I told him I was pregnant, but he didn't believe it was his. My parents tolerated me for the first few months of the pregnancy, but before long, my father was his old self and kicked me out and told me to let my N word friends to take care of me. He said, "You can go live under a bridge for all I care."

It was no secret he was prejudiced back then, and he proved it by hiding my half-black son away for the first few years of his life. My son became a master at puzzles while tucked away in the house that was completely covered by large trees. I would go visit him several times a week always when my father wasn't home. I recall a time when I was hiding behind a tree under an open window, and I could hear Brian calling out mommy. My father told him you don't have a mommy. I was livid and made sure he knew it by leaving him a threatening note after my visit that day. On the piece of cardboard that I grabbed from the stack of things to burn near the Franklin stove, I scrawled out my disgust and anger to my father. My mother had no idea I was leaving him this message of wrath. I told him I heard what he said and if he didn't give me my son back, I would have my junkie friends blow up his truck. I made sure to twist the knife by signing it: Your un-Catholic daughter.

I found out that threat ended up at the police station just in case I followed through. As I advanced in my pregnancy, I ended up staying with an older couple that lived a few streets away from my parents. Terry and Jay were heroin addicts, and they had no problem taking me in to be the live-in babysitter for the young son they neglected. He was about 4 years old and was extremely cute, but troubled just the same. He would be outside peeing in the yard doing whatever he wanted, while his mother was nodding out in the house. These two were a real piece of work. They had gotten the house from the old lady who lived there. They were her caregivers and from what I understood, they had paid $1 for the home. There were rumors that they used to tie her to the bed.

Jay was extremely attractive and used to flirt with me behind Terry's back. I liked Terry although I didn't respect her much, but with all my screwed-up actions, who was I to judge. I didn't mess around with her man at least not until several years later when she was a complete mess sleeping around with everyone.

This house was a big, brick home with two large pillars on the porch. They had two dogs: a German Shepherd named King and a Doberman Pinscher. They used to leave me in the house to take care of the meth customers that would come to buy drugs. I was very pregnant by this time, and those dogs protected me more than once. When an angry customer would return for a refund after buying a bag of crank that was cut too much, the dogs would chase them off. It was rough living there, but being almost ready to give birth my options were few. The house was infested with fleas, and they used to bite me terribly. I was so naïve that I would spray my legs with Raid to keep them off me. I never thought of the chemicals seeping into my skin.

There was a lady named Patty that used to come buy speed from me. One day she came, and I was crying because I knew I couldn't bring a new baby into that house with the drugs and the fleas. She told me not to worry that her oldest son was moving out and going to his grandmother's, and she would have an empty room by the time my son was born. I was scheduled for my second C section on September 13th, 1985; this was also a Friday. Both sons were born on Friday the 13th and I believed my life was on a bad path. I was very relieved when Patty came to pick me up from the hospital after the birth of my second son, Mark. They had a really nice house and her husband had a good job even though they were both chronic meth users. They gave me a freshly painted room with wooden floors.

Chapter 5

Pregnant Again

I had the bassinet from my mother, the one Brian had slept in when he was born. My baby boy was beautiful. He was the best baby, never fussed. I would rock him back and forth on my knees and sing him the same songs I had sang to Brian two years earlier. I don't think he ever cried for the first four months. I had a special bond with him because of the heartbreak of not having my first son. Mark became my everything. He was the one good thing I had going for me.

With no chance of employment, the next step was applying for welfare. When I got my first booklets of food stamps, I had no idea what to buy. My first real shopping trip I ended up buying a lot of junk. I came home with M&Ms and potato skins. I had no idea what to buy, how to cook, or how to shop. Patty had to help me with the next trip to the store. I was able to pay them

$200 a month for rent and helped with the food bill. They in turn kept me supplied in speed and prescriptions.

I hadn't really done pills that much, but when I was at Terry's, she introduced me to doctor shopping. She had me go to the doctor's office with my Medicaid card and get Ativan and Xanax. She might have got the first prescription from me, but anything else after that I kept. Patty and Chuck had Soma. I didn't care for them much either way, but never turned them down. (Note: *I have to say that most of the people I've written about so far are dead now and it's not my intention to badmouth them; it's just the truth of what I experienced and it's no secret.*) Everyone in Riverside that was in the drug scene knows what everyone else was doing back then in the early 80s. After my abduction, I was far beyond my years than my peers, so I gravitated towards the older crowd. Patty and I would stay up for days. She had a young daughter who was neglected when Patty would crash out for days at a time. I would take her with me to town and try to keep her occupied while Patty slept. She would run around the house slamming all the cabinet doors trying to wake her mom up. It was a vicious cycle of drugs and sleep. I had Mark, so I didn't have the luxury of crashing out for days and I wasn't taking pills like Patty. One day Patty's sister, Terri called. When Patty told her I was living there, she said, "Why is that scumbag there?" I grabbed the phone and cursed her out. She came to my house a few days later and changed her tune when she came to my room and saw my baby. She asked me who the father was and when I told her, she said, "Mike just dropped me off." I hadn't seen Mike since I gave birth, but I had to file for child support because I was collecting welfare. Terri and I became inseparable.

She was just as crazy as me, but on a different level. She had a different set of criminal skills. She was a forger and would go out at night and steal mail from mailboxes. She would get people's new credit cards and activate them by phone. The security measures were more lenient back then, so this was not hard to do. She also stole checks and would cash them at drive-thru banks. I knew she had already had Diane sign checks and she got busted, so I knew better than to sign my name. She tried to get me to do it, but my street smarts taught me better. One morning she came bursting into my room and tossed a bag on my bed full of lingerie from Victoria Secret. She informed me we were going out shopping. She had a bunch of credit cards and I was game for anything. We strapped Mark into the car seat and took off for days. We rented rooms and bought drugs. She purchased a diamond ring engagement set and gave me the band. We later pawned it when the money ran out. She was also taking cash advances out from the stolen credit cards.

On one occasion, we got dressed up and drove over to Philadelphia to Jeweler's Row. Once inside the jewelry store, the door automatically locked behind us and we looked at each other giving it a second thought. We decided it was worth the risk and made our purchases. I was good at running game and joked around with the cashier stating how angry my husband would be when the bill came in the mail. She laughed and so did we as we were let out of the store with our Ill-gotten gains. That was one of many schemes I was involved in with Terri.

I had another friend named Tammy, and she was absolutely beautiful. She had long, black hair with long, flowing curls and a really nice body. She had grown up in Virginia in a strict Christian family with her sister Lisa. Tammy was just as much of a risk taker as I was. She came along for that trip to Philadelphia. I had a special bond with Tammy. I loved her like a sister. She knew the truth about Jesus, and we would stay up high on speed and talk about getting our lives on the right track one day. There were only a handful of people who I really considered my friend, and Tammy was on the top of the list. I had fun with Terri, but I knew I could not trust her all the way because if it came down to me or her going to jail, she would throw me under the bus. She had a lot of enemies in Riverside. She was a thief and had stolen purses from a woman in the bar. Her friend list was very short. We would wait for her mom to fall asleep and steal the car then go out for days. Her mom would blame me, but it was always her idea. She had been doing it way before she met me. Terri didn't start doing drugs till she was 25. Her father died of cancer; he had holes in his head. She was daddy's girl and when he passed away, she just went off the deep end. She was fun to hang around although she was like an Amazon woman. She was tall and loud, and you knew it when she walked into a room. If there was a guy she liked and thought was attractive, she would jack them up against the wall and kiss them. Everyone would laugh, and some of the guys after drinking all night would hook up with her.

Terri's sister Patty, who I lived with previously, ended up splitting up with her husband and moved back with Terri and her mom with her kids. Terri's mom's name was Rose and even though she would get mad at us for ripping and running, she always made me feel welcome in her home. She was a great cook and I ate many meals with the family. She taught me how to cook spaghetti and laughed when I walked away from the pot without stirring the pasta. She knew I loved her fruit salad that was full of honeydew and cantaloupe. She went out of her way over the years to make sure she made it for me when I would visit.

They became my family, and I was glad to have someone that treated me like a human being. I made weekly trips to my parents' house trying to avoid my father at all costs. I went to see Brian and bring him gifts. My little brother, Patrick was also there, and I was very close to him. I always made sure I had something to bring them. I was trying to make up for the fact that I had left my son. It was the hardest thing I ever did, but I knew deep down he was better off with them. I was an active user, and there was no way a court would ever give me custody in the condition I was in. He was content where he was, and he was safe. If I wanted to take him for a walk around the block or back to the river, I had to leave Mark at the house. They were afraid I was going to take off with him, but I had no intention of tearing him away from the home he knew. I would sit out in the backyard with him and watch him run around with his curly hair. My heart broke every time I had to leave him there. It didn't affect him when he was younger, but that would change as he got older. One of my biggest regrets was giving him up instead of getting my life together.

We ran together for months. Patty was not happy that I had become partners in crime with her sister. Her family had become my family, and I spent all my holidays over there and ate dinner at her mom's house a lot. I actually felt more love from them than I did my own family. My siblings had pretty much disowned me at that point. My older brother, Eddie, seemed to hate me. He was so embarrassed of me when I first came home from being abducted, we had words a few times. After that he never spoke to me again. I saw him a few times at a party here or there, but he completely ignored me. I spoke to my sisters on and off, but I was on my own at that point and just kept my distance. My sisters were always fighting with each other over something or another, and it was always two against one and I just kept to myself. I didn't want to get caught up in the gossip and slander of family disputes. I lasted at Patty's till Mark was eight months old then it was time to go. They had enough of my running around with Terri. I ended up renting a room at a friend's house; her name was Betty. She was actually dating George, the guy I had dated years earlier. She had six kids and let me rent a nice, big room. I was paying her about $200 a month.

Once I left Patty's, I slowed down on the speed and started drinking a lot. Captain Morgan and Coke became my new addiction. I just kept myself numb to mask the pain of family rejection and the loss of Brian. I took Mark everywhere I went, and everyone loved him. He was a really good baby and never gave me any problems. He was content to sit in his umbrella stroller, while I walked around town getting drunk with my friends. I had a good friend, Dave, and we hung out acting ridiculous, laughing loud and running the streets. Terri would come pick me up, and we would cruise around drinking and yelling out the car window at the cute guys. She would buy an eight pack of Budweiser and slam them down real fast. I would tolerate it for a while, but when she drove crazy, I would make her drop me off because I had Mark in the car. My life just continued on this path of debauchery. I was doctor shopping now, putting my lying skills to work at every doctor in town that took Medicaid. Back then everything was handwritten in your chart, and the doctors did not know if you were going somewhere else. Mixing alcohol with the pills was becoming the norm for me. I know that I must have had angels protecting us because I was always in rare form. Riverside was just a big party town; it seemed like everyone was screwed up on something and with a bar on almost every corner it wasn't hard to find the next party or hangout.

We all spent a lot of time near the tracks where the train bridge was. At any given time, you would walk back and pass different groups of party people hanging out. I remember when I was about ten, I heard about a guy that was murdered back there. Years later, I found out the story, and I knew the guy's brother that was killed. His name was Phil and apparently, he had snitched on someone for something. He was back at the tracks that night and was ambushed by a group of guys. They beat him and filled his pockets with rocks and threw him off the train bridge into the Delaware River. They were caught and arrested. They went to jail, but all of them eventually got out.

Leave it to me to hook up with one of the killers a few years later. I had a good way of finding and attaching myself to the lowest of the low because that was what I thought of myself. I was no better than the next person when it came to a sinful lifestyle. I stayed at Betty's for at least a year. There were times when she wouldn't pay the electricity bill, and we used coolers and candles. We got along pretty good. George had a friend he used to bring over named Eric. He was a black guy, and we flirted a bit. I knew he was married and had a few daughters, but I had no morals and hooked up with him for about a week.

I eventually lost interest in Eric, plus with his family living right down the street I stopped seeing him. It wasn't long before I began to feel that familiar sickening feeling in the morning. I did my best to ignore the fact that I was no longer getting my period. The last thing I wanted was to be pregnant with a third child. I hid it for as long as I could, but I began to show in the 5th month. I wasn't even 100% sure if Eric was the father or the other guy I was dating before him. This was my hardest pregnancy. The entire time I was pregnant I was itchy; it was maddening. I would go to my mother crying about it. She did try to help me by allowing me to take an oatmeal bath when my father wasn't home. Nothing helped, and it drove me crazy.

I was still living at Betty's house, and I was about six months pregnant when my son dropped a bowl of cheese doodles all over her floor. She was furious when she attacked me. She was a very large woman and we fought; she ended up sitting on me. Once she got off me, she told me to find somewhere else to live. There was an old man next door named Ray, and he had a backroom. He let me stay about a month, but when I refused to sleep with him, he kicked me out.

There was a place a few towns over in Riverton called Emergency Services. I went there, and they put me in a place called the Clover Motel in Maple Shade. It was far from Riverside, and I was isolated from everyone. Terri had just gotten out of federal prison and was working at a hotel near there, so she would come see me. She got caught one night stealing mail, while I was waiting for her in a room with Mark. She never came back, and I later found out she got busted. I would catch the bus and go to Cinnaminson and get my own room sometimes. I had taken Mike to court for child support, but he was trying to get his act together and was going to school to be a chiropractor. His uncle was his lawyer so for the first 6 years of Mark's life, I only received $10 a week. That same uncle was a prosecutor in Burlington County, so I'm sure he had some pull with the judge. It seemed like a conflict of interest to me, but who would listen. I didn't have the skills or motivation to fight it. There were a few months in between living with Patty and Betty that I had nowhere to go. I got minimal money from the state, not enough to pay for a room every night. Mike knew I was struggling to take care of his son, but never helped me. One time I was sitting in the Cinnaminson Motor Lodge and the check-out time was noon. I was watching CBN, the Christian show on T.V. As I listened to Pat Robertson pray, I asked God to please help me. I asked him for my own stable place to take my son. I had an umbrella stroller, a bag of clothes with my hair dryer and makeup with nowhere to go. I was walking down the highway crying wondering where we would sleep that night. It was shortly after that when I ran into George, and he told me Betty had the room for rent. So here I was again back in the motels with my 2-year-old son and ready to give birth again. I had a room at the Garden State Motel toward the end of my pregnancy. I had about a month to go. One day my sister came rolling in with a guy I didn't know. She had left her longtime boyfriend Billy, and was now seeing this new guy Ed. She was extremely excited and seemed to really love this guy. She informed me she was moving out, and I asked if she thought Billy would rent me a room. She said she would let me know and when she was done moving out. I moved in just a few weeks before my third scheduled C section. Billy was like a brother to me; my sister had been with him for a long time. He was actually Tammy and Lisa's uncle. One night he came into my room drunk while I was sleeping and tried to mess around with me. I was disgusted and told him to stop, especially since I was 9 months pregnant.

It was great to have a place to live right before having my baby. I gave birth to my daughter Dawn on September 11, 1987. I had another scheduled C section on a Friday. I had finally agreed to have a tubal ligation after having Dawn. They had tried to persuade me to get my tubes tied after the birth of my first son, but I refused. They actually had the paperwork ready for me to sign as if I had asked for the procedure. I'm thankful I didn't allow them to sterilize me at 16. I may have had a life of hard knocks, but my children are the biggest blessings in my life.

I was in the hospital under a different name because

when I was struggling. I had answered an ad in the newspaper about giving your baby up for adoption. I still was not sure what I was going to do. I didn't know if I could take care of another baby. The guy that placed the ad told me he had a couple that would take my baby. I was just trying to get money from him for shelter. I told him I had nowhere to live, and he sent me money by Western Union three times. I received a total of $3,000 from him. He also thought my baby was white. They would have not been interested in a mixed baby. On one of our phone calls, he sounded tired and out of sorts. He told me that he had been out shooting a 44 Magnum. He asked me if I knew what that was and quickly told me it was the largest handgun. I thought he was trying to scare me, but he had no idea who he was dealing with. He was actually a lawyer named Richard Gitelman. My parents knew I had scammed him out of thousands, and they were fearful he would come to the hospital to take my baby. A few months later, Tammy and I were napping in my living room and the news was on the TV. I was jolted from my sleep when I heard his name on the news. Richard Gitelman was a baby broker selling babies on the black market. He was from Florida and was arrested for luring a minor to Louisiana to get her baby. He was getting $50,000 for her baby. After leaving her stranded in a local motel, she called the cops and he was arrested. Right after having my daughter, my parents had come to see me in the hospital. My father actually had the nerve to offer me $100 if I let them take my baby. It disgusted me. I told them to buy me a double stroller because I was keeping my daughter with me.

I suffered terribly with postpartum depression after having Dawn. I cried all the time, and it was very difficult for me to bond with my new baby. This made me feel so guilty. She was absolutely beautiful with black, curly hair and long, pretty fingers. Like my other two children she was very well behaved and easy to care for. My drinking was out of control. We had tons of people coming and going all the time. Billy was a big drinker as well, so it was always party time. My parents didn't live too far from the apartment. It was a three-bedroom place with an attic over top of a place called Milanese Pizza. There was a stop light right outside the window, and I would see my parents waiting at the light looking up at the window. I'm sure they heard all the noise from the parties we were having. Eventually, Billy moved out and I asked the landlord if I could take over the lease. This was my first official apartment. I was thrilled, but I was so immature that I didn't do a very good job being a responsible tenant. I paid the rent, but it was a complete madhouse of drugs and alcohol. The kids were small enough not to realize what was going on. As they got a little older, I chilled out and tried to get my life right with God. As soon as I did that, everyone stopped coming over. Tammy moved in with me. She helped me with

Dawn a lot. I was grateful for her help. She had a terrible experience a few years earlier when she got pregnant. She went to have an abortion and after they administered the saline solution, she jumped off the table and ran out. She could feel her baby writhing in pain and went to the hospital. The doctors would not touch her.

Her father lived in Virginia, and they had life flight her to a Catholic hospital there. She gave birth to a little girl who was black and burnt from the abortion. When she woke up the next day, they had a picture of her baby on the table by her bed. I don't know why they would do that. I imagine it was to remind her not to do that again.

We used to sleep in the same bed, and she woke up one night in a cold sweat telling me she had a dream. She said in the dream her mother came and picked her up and took her on a ride to show her something. They drove down a long, winding road with lots of trees and green grass. They pulled up and a little girl with long black hair like Tammy's came towards the car. She was bouncing a ball. Her mother yelled at her to roll up the window and drove off. Tammy was devastated over that abortion.

I was having my own sleep issues at that time. Tammy and I were talking about Jesus and how we wanted to do better. I came under severe spiritual attack. As I would be dozing off to sleep, my ears would ring and a dark presence would hold me down on the bed. My eyes would be open, and I would be aware of where I was. I wouldn't be able to move. Some people may call it sleep paralysis, but I knew it was demonic from the pits of hell. The only way it would release me is when I was finally able to say the name of Jesus. I had opened doors to the dark side in that apartment. I had gotten a hold of a satanic bible, and a few of us had done a séance with candles. While we were doing it, my friend Dave began choking and ripped up the satanic bible.

There were plenty of dark forces in that apartment, and I wasn't equipped to get them to go. I felt like they were in the attic. I went through a battle with fear up there for a few months. I hated being alone up there. My attempt to get my life together was short-lived. I did chill out on the drugs because I loved my kids and didn't want to end up like a lot of the older moms in town who were strung out. I did, however, continue to drink. I met a girl named Missy who lived around the corner from me. Tammy moved out and I started hanging over with Missy. Her house became the new party spot. She had two young boys. We would take the kids to Riverside Park, and we would drink and play Frisbee while the kids ran around and played. We would take the kids home and give them baths and party all night. My kids were really easy and well-behaved. Missy would put her kids upstairs in a backroom with a lock on the outside of the door. They would be banging and yelling, and on several occasions, they took off their diapers and smeared poop on the walls.

It wasn't long before I gave up my apartment and rented a room from Missy. Why would I want to pay $500 in rent plus electricity when I could give her $200 and not be alone up there? Missy had a party one night, and there was a new guy there I had never seen. He was older than me and he was quiet. He just sat back watching and that was attractive to me. His name was Johnny Travea, and we started dating. I fell for him hard. We hung out every day. He was living with his brother in Willingboro but would spend the night with me a lot. I was devastated when I got a good look at his arms one day and realized this guy had a heroin habit. It was too late, I already loved him. I hated it when he took trips to Camden to buy his dope. I did my best to ignore it. He was funny and we got along well. Mark was five now and was getting ready to start kindergarten. Dawn was three.

One night we got drunk and went to this old guy's house. His name was Charlie, and he was the town drunk that fell down and got robbed a lot. We needed money, so we went to his house and robbed him. He fought back, and Johnny ended up hitting him a few times. We took off and really didn't give it a second thought. This old man was tough, and it wasn't the first time he had been robbed. Unfortunately, for me this was the time he called the cops.

Chapter 6

The Misery Continues

Mark was starting kindergarten in two days after we robbed Charlie. The day before he was to start Johnny and I had gone out and picked up all his school supplies. We were lying in bed that night when we heard a loud banging on the door. I knew the cops were heading upstairs, so I quickly took a few Xanax because if I was going to jail, I would need them. I had been taking them for a long time and withdrawal in jail was not going to be fun. They locked me up and charged me with strong armed robbery. They didn't take Johnny because Charlie didn't know who he was, and they ended up locking up another guy named Jack because they thought he was with me. I was denying the whole thing, so when I saw Jack in court, he was looking at me and asked me what was going on. I felt bad, but just shrugged my shoulders. I had a $10,000 bail with no ten percent, so I was cooling my jets for a while. I was absolutely devastated that I was going to miss out on

Mark's first day of school. Johnny got him on the bus for me and ended up taking my kids to his brother's house. His brother was married with one son. He kept them for about three days before dropping them off at my parents' house. I had no choice but to let them take care of them while I was in jail.

I was in the cell with an older black woman named Miss D. She ran the commissary, and she was the only one in there for murder. She had stabbed her abusive husband to death and received 13 years. We got along great. I was ok for the first few days, but once the Xanax wore off, I asked to see the shrink. He prescribed me lower doses, and I was able to wean comfortably. I don't know if they do that for addicts now, but this was 1991.

I remembered I used to hang out with a criminal lawyer from Cherry Hill, so I tried to get him to help me with my case. He was busy on a high-profile case that would enhance his career. It was a gruesome case in Philadelphia where a father had killed his adult daughter, dismembered her, and was boiling her on the stove. He promised to get to my case as soon as he could, so I sat in jail and adjusted the best I could. The only issue I had was with one of the guards, Miss. Johnson, who just did not like me. She took one of my away visits. The worst part of being in jail was not being with my kids. I missed them so much. My parents allowed Terri to bring them to see me.

It was so good seeing my children. I looked at Dawn and it looked like she had gained 10 pounds in two weeks. Her little legs were so chunky. My mom told me she had been eating spaghetti. I asked Mark how kindergarten was going for him and we discussed what he was learning. When it was time for them to go, it was heart wrenching to say goodbye to them.

A few times a week a group of Christian women would come to the jail and minister to the women. I hit it off with one of them; her name was Tina. She played the guitar and sang songs; she was Filipino and had long, black hair. She and her husband were bikers that used to shoot speed and she had several abortions. Now she was involved with helping women and was deeply involved in Operation Rescue. I liked her a lot and looked forward to her coming to the jail.

I was held for 30 days before my lawyer finally came to court and I got my ten percent bail. Terri's mom put up the $1,000 on Christmas at the bail bonds, and I was released. I slept at Terri's the first night and hooked up with Johnny the next day. We went and picked up my kids and checked into the Garden State Motel for a few days. After three days we ran out of money. I realized that I was tired of living like this, and I decided to call Tina's number to speak to her. She told me she would help me when I got out if I needed it, and I needed it. She picked up me and the kids and let us move into her home. Mark had to change schools, but we liked it there. It was nice, and they had a big finished garage they let us stay in. They had one other girl staying there; her name was Jeanie. We all got along, and I began seeking Jesus more. It was easier when I was living with people who served the Lord. Tina woke up early every morning, and we all had to do praise and worship while she played the guitar. She had two kids: George and Nikki.

We would go with the Operation Rescue group and block the doors to the abortion mill. They were hard-core when it came to saving the babies. They were locked up more than once due to their protesting. We went over to South Street in Philadelphia and would try to win souls for Jesus. We were witnessing for Christ and helping as many that would come into the knowledge of our savior.

I remember the first time I felt the presence of the Holy Spirit. We were in a circle praying in the living room at home and I began to feel like I was high, but in a good way. Johnny would come over to visit because I loved him. I was really trying to be good and did not want to fall back into sin and old patterns. I had decided to change my life, and that was my focus. This is what was in my heart, but the strongholds were too strong to resist. After about six weeks, I stayed out all night in a room with Johnny. When

Tina found out, she kicked me out. She told me, "I'm not running a hotel. I'm here to help people who want to serve God."

With nowhere to go, I ended up going to the Social Services building in Mt. Holly to apply for emergency housing. They were putting homeless mothers in different motels, and I ended up getting a room at the Burlington Motel. It was away from Riverside and that was a good thing. With this move, Mark had to transfer schools yet again. This was his third school. I wasn't supposed to have anyone staying in the room with me, but me being me and being a master rule breaker, Johnny came along for the ride. He helped me with the kids and always made sure we had what we needed. We went behind the rooms, and he built the kids a little fort out of scrap wood that was laying around. The people who ran the motel were nice to me. I never had issues with them. They actually had picnic tables set up with umbrellas and we would all sit out, drink and talk. I would go to the organizations that helped out with Christmas gifts for the kids. Johnny would ride Mark to school on his bike for me. He didn't have a car. He would thumb it everywhere like me or we would all catch the bus together since the motel was right on Route 130. We stayed there till spring, and I found a nice apartment that accepted people on welfare. The state paid my security deposit and we moved in. It was super nice. I wouldn't have to push my laundry down the street to the laundromat anymore. The laundry room was right downstairs. I might have been poor and struggling, but I was a clean freak and kept my kids and house clean.

We loved it at Hillcrest apartments. We settled in and I made friends with a few of the people in the complex. It was always easy to gravitate towards the people who liked to hang out and party. There was a girl across the street named Chris who had a daughter Dawn's age, so they played together while we drank and laid out in the sun. Lots of kids there, so my kids had fun and we were able to relax for a while and enjoy a stable place to live. Johnny started staying out more and more not coming home, and I was getting sick of it. We had a few physical fights and he was starting to get on my nerves. One day, I saw a girl moving in that I had been locked up with. Her name was Kim. She was a tall, blonde chick with spider web tattoos on her elbows. She liked to hang out with bikers. We started hanging out drinking together. She had just given birth to a baby boy a few months earlier. She neglected that little boy by leaving him in the back room for hours at a time while she got high. This was the early 90s and crack was Chris' drug of choice. I tried it a few times but didn't like how it made me feel. I stuck to drinking. I did manage to get myself a little part-time job at deli close to the apartments. I opened a bank account, and Chris was watching Dawn for me. She stole my bank book and took $100 for crack. After she stole from me, I left her alone for a while, and Kim and

I started hanging out again.

One day I was over at Kim's apartment when she said her baby's father was on the way. When he walked through the door, I was surprised how good looking he was. Right away, we hit it off when he told me he had been to California. We had something in common.

Kim not only smoked crack, but she also did heroin. She started taking off with Johnny to go to Camden and buy dope, and George, her baby's dad and I were left behind together. I didn't mind because he was beautiful with really long, straight hair, and he was interesting. He had stories like me. I never revealed my abduction to anyone. I had buried it somewhere deep and continued to drown it in alcohol. It wasn't long before George and I were sneaking around. He wasn't with Kim anymore. He just came to see the kid. He wasn't even sure if he was the baby's biological father, but he was trying to do the right thing.

We started dating around Christmas, and I finally got up the nerve to break up with Johnny. He came home on his birthday, New Year's Day 1992 and I told him to leave. He was devastated and kept banging on the door. I was done. I did feel bad, but I was moving on with George now. It was clear we couldn't stay there and have peace, so we decided to leave the state. We thought about going to Los Angeles, but the Rodney King riots were going on. We settled on

Florida, and I began to pack and get rid of everything I didn't need.

As our relationship started to grow, I explained to him that I wanted to get right with God. He listened and heard what I was saying, so we tried hard not to sleep together. It didn't work. He asked me to marry him and I said yes. I never wanted to marry anyone, but there was just something about him that made me say yes. Actually, I couldn't believe he wanted to marry me. He was a few years younger than me, and I had three kids already. He was just as dysfunctional as me and we headed down south to tie the knot. My friend Dave drove us to Philadelphia to the Greyhound Bus Station. We boarded a bus to Orlando with a bunch of bags and his duffel bag full of albums. It was exciting and new, and I was ready for a clean start. I knew I liked it down in Florida because it was warm and the palm trees were beautiful. We checked into a weekly rental called the Howard Vernon Motel on Colonial Drive in Orlando. It was nothing fancy, just cheap enough to be a starting place. Across the street was Lake Dot. We settled in and went exploring where everything was. We went Downtown to Church Street Station and purchased a cheap set of sterling wedding bands.

We applied for our marriage license and on Brian's Birthday, May 13th, 1992, we got married by the Justice of the Peace. Mark and Dawn were our witnesses. George found work pretty quickly, and I stayed home to take care of the kids. Another move, another school, Mark was starting school number four.

Not too long into our marriage, I quickly learned George was the jealous type. I had no idea and did not see any signs before we were married. One day, he came home to find me hanging out with a neighbor guy drinking beer. He ran full force and kicked out the living room window. We were living in a small efficiency apartment. I was shocked by his behavior. I had never seen him angry, I told him we were just hanging out. The guy took off and George had to pay to replace the window. Mr. Ho from the office was not too happy; he was not about to put up with a lot of crap from us.

One thing I learned is that George had his own baggage. He came from a family of alcoholics. When he was five, he came home from school to find the ambulance at his house taking his mother out on a stretcher because she had passed away. She fell asleep with a cigarette, which caused the house to catch on fire and died in a fire. His father was a drinker and by the time George was nine, he was stealing drinks from the adults and getting drunk. We had drunk together a lot since we met, but I never saw him get nasty until two months after we were married. It was the 4th of July and I had gone to a local fairground swap meet on the bus and found him a record player for his albums. When I got back, he had already started drinking. He was drinking 151 Rum. We had planned to go downtown for the fireworks with the kids that night, but as the day progressed, it was clear he was getting really intoxicated. He was listening to his Neil Diamond album and crying. It was the song, *"We're Coming to America."* I didn't like it and it would not end well.

He passed out early and when I tried to wake him up, he was nasty. He was cursing and yelling at me. I had promised the kids we would go downtown to Lake Eola and watch the fireworks. He was far too intoxicated to come along, and I didn't want to be around him acting like that. So, I decided to go by myself with the kids. As the kids and I started walking away, he was hanging out the window calling me names. I was not the type of woman who was going to take orders from anyone, married or not. After what I had been through, I was not going to allow anyone to treat me like crap without a fight. I wasn't that 15-year-old girl anymore. I continued to walk away while he was still yelling and carrying on. The kids and I went to the fireworks as planned and when we returned home, he was still on the warpath.

He had destroyed the place. He cut up a bunch of my photos. My suitcase was floating in Lake Dot. He spit on me, and I ended up calling the cops on him. Florida had just passed a law that if there was any violence at all in a domestic disturbance that the offender was to be locked up for a cool-off period. This came about because of a recent case where they released the offender and he ended up killing the girl. I told them he didn't hit me, but he spit on me. He did go into the lake to get my suitcase. They considered spitting on someone an assault, so there I was crying while my new husband of two months was carted off to jail.

By that time, I was getting more child support from Mike for Mark, and I was collecting benefits. I was making ends meet, but the loss of George's income made it a little difficult. George's roofing was under the table, but now I was on my own till he was released. I was devastated.

Our room had a phone, so I was able to talk to him a few times a week. He was getting harassed by the biggest black guy in jail who was there for murder. I called some lawyers, but there was no way to get him out with the new law anytime soon. There were a few times when I hitchhiked to the jail to visit him while my neighbor friend watched the kids. He was locked up for six weeks. I was happy when he got out. He was a smoker and hadn't smoked in six weeks, and that was the first thing he wanted. I was disappointed, but he started smoking again. We stayed at Howard Vernon for about eight months. We had more fights and George broke more windows. He then had to pay for them to get fixed.

The opportunity came for us to take over the lease for a nice apartment on the other side of town. We moved and Mark started another new school, school number five. There was a small strip mall right near the apartments, and I got a job at a little place called Kathy's Wings & Subs. First thing they had me do was cut up celery. It was a fun job. I really liked working. We had kegs of beer there and the owner didn't care if we drank. The wings were the best I've ever had. He named the place after his daughter Kathy. She was a spoiled brat that was smoking crack and she used to come in the shop and take money from the cash register. I worked as much as possible, and George stayed home and took care of the kids.

The people who let us take over the lease wanted the apartment back, so we had to move. I was working so I was able to get us another place at Forest Village apartments. It was nice and had a pool. Poor Mark had to start school number six. I was working the night shift, so I had all day to spend with Dawn. Our bond had begun to grow since we lived in Florida. She was adorable with long, curly hair and I had lots of pretty hats for her. We would catch the bus everywhere, and I always got so many compliments about her beauty. We were getting closer, and I was glad that I no longer dealt with the feelings that it was so hard for me.

Working always gave me a sense of purpose. We spent a lot of our days in the pool hanging out with the neighbors.

George worked in the day and I worked nights. We were still having some issues. It's hard to make a relationship work when you're drinking and don't have God. We only lasted in Florida a little over a year before returning to Jersey. We rented a U-Haul and drove back. I missed Brian terribly and was happy to see him when we got back.

I missed the sunshine and warm weather of Florida, but I missed Brian more. He was the best thing I had going for me in Jersey. I suffered from depression in the winter, so it was always my dream to live in a warm, tropical climate. We stored all our stuff in a shed at my parents' house and didn't have anywhere to live. We stayed at a motel for a while, but quickly ran out of money. George's family lived in Burlington and they let us stay with them for a little bit, but they got fed up with the fighting. I too got fed up and ended up leaving and going into a shelter in Willingboro. It was a really nice house with one other family there with me. She was a black lady and her two kids, and she ran the place. I had a nice big room. I stayed awhile, then I was moved to a woman and kids shelter called the Mustard Seed in Mt. Holly.

I was devastated that my husband wasn't able to take care of us. He was selfish and was out drinking and doing drugs. I was determined to get my own place and I applied for a job in the town his father lived in. Roebling was a small town and I seemed to fit right in. I got myself a job at the local Shop-N- Bag as a deli worker. I had a little experience, but not too much. I was a fast learner and did well there. The lady who trained me was retiring in a few months. By working there, I was able to afford a small two-bedroom apartment. The kids and I moved in, but of course my husband came crawling back. I let him come because I still loved him. So, another new school for Mark and now Dawn was ready for kindergarten. They both started at Roebling Elementary School.

One of my customers from the Shop-N-Bag named Wanda was the local babysitter. She was nice and inexpensive and agreed to watch my kids when I needed her. George was working again. He was roofing with one of his friends. We started going to Bible study and both stopped drinking for nine months. Kindergarten was a little difficult for Dawn at first because there were not many mixed kids. She had to adjust to being different than others. One day near Thanksgiving, the kids had an art project to make the construction paper turkey where you trace your hand. When the teacher handed out the paper, she gave all the kids pink paper and handed Dawn brown. She came home crying to me. Needless to say, I went to the school and addressed the issue. Over the years, she faced many battles due to the fact she was mixed.

Springtime was approaching and it was time for the local carnival. My friend Dave came over and we went to the carnival, and I fell off the wagon and got drunk. That was the green light for George to start drinking as well, and it was all downhill from there. He began staying out all night and that was the one thing I hated. I had been promoted to Deli manager and got a raise. I was getting more child support from Mike because he was now a practicing Chiropractor. I began to abuse codeine cough syrup. There was a doctor who would give me 16-ounce bottles of Phenergan with codeine. I had taken it over the years, but now it was becoming an issue. The only reason I could take it without getting sick was because it had Phenergan for nausea. I couldn't take pain pills because they made me sick. That was a blessing in disguise. I was still getting Xanax.

One day I ran into Tammy at the Courthouse in Mt. Holly, while in court with Mike. She looked great. She told me she had a son now and her husband was a doctor, but she was separated. She was dancing and making a bunch of money. She took me to the mall and bought me a new bathing suit and some clothes. George got caught driving without a license and was locked up. I didn't care at that point. Tammy came and picked me up one night, and we went to Philadelphia to party. She was living a very fast-paced life. I had settled down to take care of my kids. We went out drinking and flirting with cops. I drank so much that I blacked out and knocked over a table of drinks at Dave & Busters. I didn't even remember; she told me the next day. We planned to go out again in a couple weeks, and I couldn't get ahold of her. On June 17th, 1994, I was watching the news when they were chasing O.J Simpson in the white Bronco on television when the phone rang. Tammy was found dead at the Cinnaminson Motor Lodge from a heroin overdose.

The news of Tammy's overdose completely shattered me. This was only the second death of someone close to me. The first one was Jay Falcone, who was previously Terry's man. I lived with them when I was pregnant with Mark. Well, when I was still living over top of the pizza place, I had started writing to Jay in Trenton State Prison. Terry had become completely unhinged and was not being faithful to him. I hitchhiked to the prison a few times to see him. He was really attractive, a tall Italian man with salt and pepper hair. He was tan and had a large castle tattoo that covered his entire back. I had always been attracted to him but would not cross the line because I liked Terry. After seeing her actions when he was locked up, I was ready to cross the line. She didn't care for him, so I thought he was free game. I would go into the prison drunk. I don't know how I got away with that. I remember on one of my visits that I gave him the necklace I was wearing, and he gave me his flannel shirt to take home. I was getting ready to leave the visitation area when the guards swooped on me. They thought I was trying to smuggle something out. That was the last time I went up. He was released shortly after that, and he came to spend the weekend with me. Terry had moved to Hollywood, Florida with their son and he was going to see them for two weeks then come back to me. He never made it back. He went to buy coke from the Puerto Ricans, and they beat him to death with a baseball bat. He had a ton of gold on him, and they robbed him and killed him. I was devastated and it took me a long time to get over it.

So, now here was Tammy, my spiritual sister. We were supposed to get it right one day. She had been out with her ex-husband, and she had won a bikini contest and had a bunch of money. They got a room and got high and she died. He just left her there and took all the money and the drugs. I wondered where she was. Was she in hell because she died doing drugs? I had lost a bunch of friends from drugs, but it didn't affect me like Tammy. Diane had gone off the deep end, the one who first got me partying. She ended up dying with AIDS from what I heard. The last time I saw her I was living at Missy's and she was hitchhiking back from Camden. She had abscesses on her neck from shooting up.

There were at least 20 other people from school that were dead from drugs and alcohol. It was an epidemic. I was glad I had stopped with the hardcore drugs when my kids were young. I didn't want to die. I had tried dope a few times since, but it made me sick. Puking and scratching weren't enjoyable for me. They had a private service for Tammy. I heard her new husband was devastated. He was left to raise his son without his beautiful wife. She told me she left him because he was high society, and his friends were all doctors and she was uncomfortable around them. She was untamable. She couldn't settle down and relax. She thrived on the excitement of the fast lane, and it cost her her life. She was only 25 when she passed away. Her sister was absolutely destroyed. We lost touch for many years after Tammy died, but God had plans for Lisa and I further down the road.

Right after I lost Tammy, George started doing heroin. I couldn't believe it. I had kicked him out of the apartment because he was staying out all night. His sister called me one day and said he was passed out in the basement with a needle hanging out of his arm. I was disgusted. I hated New Jersey with a passion. It was cold, depressing, and seemed to have a dark cloud over it. I was always depressed; everyone was addicted, people were dying, and I was fed up. I lasted at my job for over a year, but my personal life was falling apart again, and I decided I was going to take my kids and head back to Florida. I didn't want to be around if George was doing heroin. I wasn't ready for another death. I went to see Brian before I left, and he begged me not to go. I can still see him crying asking me to stay. My next big regret was leaving him again.

Chapter 7

Young and Selfish

When you are young and selfish, you fail to realize the impact that you can have on a child. I tried to get him back while I was working as a deli manager. I was sober and filed for visitation on my terms. I took my parents to court, and they had a lawyer and I didn't. The judge I was in front of had just lost his brother, and I was the one who made his lunch meat platter for the funeral. My parent's lawyer told the judge how I was unstable, and how I lived in at least 18 different places. He explained that I was a drug user and drinker. When it came to my turn, the judge asked me where I worked. He told the lawyer he wasn't concerned about my past; he wanted to know what I was doing now. I told him I was sober and working at the deli. I told him I had two other children, and I just wanted to have visitation with my son at my house. He agreed and gave me every other weekend and Wednesday. I was thrilled. I got my son the next weekend and took him down the shore. I still have a picture of him feeding me grapes on the beach.

The next time he came, he didn't want to follow the same rules as Mark and Dawn, and he got angry at me and called my dad to come get him. He didn't want to come anymore. It doesn't make a difference either way. I loved him so much, and I have a hard time forgiving myself for leaving him again. Going back to Florida was a difficult decision, but I had to go. I was a bit nervous going down alone with the kids, but I had a couple thousand dollars when we arrived in Orlando again. This time I checked into the Econo Lodge. It had a bar attached to it, and it was only a few weeks before my money began dwindling. I was putting in applications everywhere and it was hard to get a job while staying in the motel. I eventually ran out of money, and we ended up in the Salvation Army Women's Shelter. My kids were so good. They never complained. They were just content to be with me. It was really nice in the shelter. They had everything we needed. It was a few days before Christmas when we got there, and they had all kinds of stuff for the kids. They took us to dinner at Medieval Times. We stayed in the shelter till the end of February. I went to file my taxes, and I had no idea I was eligible to get over $3,000 back. It was the first job on the books I had in a while. Kathy's Wings paid me in cash.

When we left the Salvation Army, I ended up renting a

room from a lady who owned the tanning spa I used to go to. It was a nice big house and I got to tan for free after that. I paid her for six months in advance. We had a nice room and the kids were happy. I contacted George a few months later, and Sherry, the lady I was renting from, said he could come and stay with us. He came down and it was ok for a while, but he got angry one night when we were supposed to go out together. He changed his mind and I went anyway. Once again, I came home and he had destroyed my stuff. He called me names and kicked me in the ear. Sherry was attracted to him, so I was asked to leave.

My friend Candy had a trailer, and she let me stay there with her. It was actually down the street from Kathy's Wings, so I ended up working there again. The landlord of the trailer park found out we were staying there, and I had to leave. I was devastated again with nowhere to go. I stored all my stuff in Candy's shed and ended up on the bus back to Jersey. Greyhound lost my luggage with all of our possessions, including all my and the kids' new clothes from income tax as well as my poems that I had written over the years. I ended up back in Jersey with nothing and again, my life was a complete mess. Here I was dragging these kids back and forth to Florida. Mark changed schools so many times I stopped counting. I ended up getting back together with Johnny, and George ended up going to Hawaii. I stayed in Jersey with Johnny for a while and just lived in motels with the kids. We moved from motel to motel, with no stable place to call home.

My kids had everything they needed, except a stable mother, who could not seem to get herself together. I was like a wave in the ocean being tossed back and forth. Would I ever just stop and grow up? Not yet.

As I write these pages and try to remember the events of my hectic life, it all just seems to be jumbled together. My kids were getting older, and they had been through a lot already. More than any kid should go through. My oldest son was at least stable with my parents. My father kept a little black book and wrote down everything I ever did to the best of his knowledge. Having that book now with the dates would help me so much, but I don't have the nerve to ask for it.

Johnny and I stayed in Jersey for a while until we decided to go to Florida. We went right back to the same Econo Lodge as before. With the bar attached to the motel, of course we were drinking. We weren't even there two weeks before we had a big fight, and he was taken to jail. Just like the times before, I was running out of money. I checked back into the Salvation Army Women's Shelter and waited for Johnny to be released. I managed to save enough to move into a small house in the middle of the hood. I got a job at a local bar.

I remember walking home one night after closing and it was very late. There was a group of guys that drove by me slowly, yelling at me. One of them threw a bottle of soda at me. I was terrified and shaking. It was only by the grace of God that I saw a church van dropping someone off and ran up and asked the driver to please let me in because I was being followed. He took me home. We had to get out of that neighborhood because it was unsafe. My boss at the bar helped me get into a nice complex near Universal Studios called Summerfield. This place was super nice and it had two large pools. The kids had a lot of fun there.

Johnny was eventually released, and we lasted about eight months before we broke up. He moved in with another woman. I met a friend who needed to rent a room; her name was Kim. She was a security guard for Universal Studios. She was always giving us free passes to get in the park, and if we saw her when we went, she would get us to the front of the line. I had quit my job because it was too far, and I got tired of taking the bus. Working in a bar wasn't the best place for me. Eventually, I was unable to keep up with the bills. We moved around to a few more places before I decided to go back to Jersey.

It was late 1997, and by now we got back and checked into another room at the Northern Motor Lodge in Cinnaminson. Terri used to come see me there. The maintenance guy, Rudy, was always hanging around and we would chill out and drink beer. Crack was in full swing by then, and it seemed like everyone was doing it, including Terri. I couldn't understand how they enjoyed getting all wacked out, peeking out the window and picking up crumbs off the floor trying to smoke pieces of plaster. I had tried it with Chris years earlier, out of a can, but wasn't really interested. That was about to change when Terri came to the motel and we were all drinking. She had some crack and asked me if I wanted to try it. This time it was a long glass tube she called a stem. I took a hit, and the next year of my life was consumed with this wicked drug.

One night I was hanging out with Rudy, and he had a few friends with him and they were getting high. One of the friend's names was Jim. Jim had a lot of drugs and money. He had recently been released from prison. He was a getaway driver for a guy who robbed a few gas stations and killed a guy. Jim had also hidden the bloody knife and clothes. Upon release, he inherited a million dollars from his uncle, and he was blowing through it like a madman. Leave it to me to hook up with him. We had the kids in one room and we stayed in another. I went on a binge and lost a ton of weight. We would just order food and give the kids money to go to the store and get food. Dawn was now 10 and Mark was 12. He had so much money that we would take the kids and check into fancy rooms for a few nights. The Cherry Hill Hyatt was hundreds of dollars a night. One of our favorite places to do was a place called The Inn of

The Dove that had theme rooms. We stayed in the Ice Castle room and the Kings Court room.

He showered me with gifts and jewelry. It was nice not to worry about money for a while, but the cost was deep. I was literally becoming a shell of a person. I was now only 98 pounds. He was starting to sneak around at night. I caught him coming in the room in the middle of the night with a black mask on his face. I had no idea what he was doing. On one occasion, he gave me $1,000 and ordered a limo. He told me to go get the kids and take them shopping at the mall. I later found out why; he was messing around with my friend Carol, and they had snuck off to another hotel. I was growing weary of the drug life. My kids had to know we were getting high. I felt so guilty and knew it was all about to come to an end.

After a long night of getting high, I told him I was done. He chose to continue and headed back to Camden for more drugs. I didn't see him anymore after that. I still had a habit and didn't stop completely, but it had been a year and it was taking a toll on me and my kids. I was back to struggling again. One night Mark was crying and really upset when we had to leave the hotel that we were staying in. I broke down and promised him I would get it together and that he would attend the same high school for the next four years. This lifestyle was not good for my kids. I had to do something different, better, if not for me, definitely for them.

I met an older guy, Dave, in court. He picked us up and moved us to a room in Bordentown. I began to do better and got a job at the Bordentown deli. We moved to a few different motels in the area until we ended up at the Bordentown Motel. I got a job cleaning rooms, and then I got a better job at a place called Hogback Deli. I did great there. I worked really hard and it paid well. My boss, George, was a classical pianist. He had a bunch of young boys working there, and I was the only woman for a while. This place made the best and biggest hoagies. We had to cut trash cans full of lettuce and giant tubs of onions and tomatoes. He had the rolls special made. I destroyed my arms working there. I ended up getting carpal tunnel. I kept pushing forward because seeing my son break down that night had motivated me to do better. I was determined to keep my promise that he would only go to one high school. First step was getting us out of the motel. I saved up enough to move us into a complex called Eagle Rock. My boss had been good to me. George trusted me to open and close, and he used to slip me $50 bills as a bonus for working hard.

He was physically sick and had to take a trip to New York for medical care. He left me in charge while he was gone. We had a big meat delivery, and the bill came to $1,300. I paid Boars Head and had the receipt. After the first few days after moving into our new apartment, I went to work and he called me in the office. He asked me where the $1,300 was, and I told him I paid the meat bill. He accused me of practicing his signature and fired me. I had no idea what he was talking about, but I just left crying. I walked home, and Dawn tried to comfort me telling me everything would be ok. She was almost 13 and Mark was 15. I couldn't believe it. I was absolutely devastated. I applied for unemployment and got it because he had no proof that I did anything wrong. I later found out that the boys were practicing his signature. I took the entire summer off and collected unemployment and went fishing almost every day. I was still drinking, but not as much as I used to. My neighbor let me practice driving her car and finally, at age 38, I got my driver's license. I never wanted it before because I was a lush and didn't want to drink and drive. There was too much risk that with my drinking, I'd do the unimaginable and risk killing myself or my kids.

I started working at the Ace Hardware down the street. I was doing great and the owner liked me. The manager felt threatened by me and tried to set me up for theft. I was not stealing. I was moving forward in the right direction. I was let go again and now I was fed up. It must have been the enemy using other people to make me fail. I was strong willed, a hard worker and smart. I can do something on my own to make money, I thought, and I would do just that.

Chapter 8
Making Changes

In 1999, I got my income tax check and purchased my first car. I was alone when I purchased it, and it had an oil leak. It was a Chrysler LeBaron. I knew nothing about cars, so these guys took advantage of me. The engine seized up the second day I drove it. They did swap out for another Chrysler LeBaron. This one was a convertible. I had nothing but problems with the car.

Now that I had transportation, I started my own cleaning business. I had business cards made up and called it *B & D Cleaning and Organizing*. This was something Dawn and I could do together. She was like me when it came to being clean and putting everything in its place. I put a few cards in the local laundromat, and that was all it took. I got my first customer, and it was all word of mouth after that. Our business quickly grew.

I found out my husband, George, was back in New Jersey after spending time in Hawaii. I was curious about how he was doing, so I called him. He was happy to hear from me and came to see us. He wasn't looking that good. He had cut his hair short and he had smelly feet. I had really chilled out on my drinking at this point, but I was abusing the codeine cough syrup. He was drinking hard liquor and driving. One day he stood in my kitchen and guzzled a half pint of vodka. He started crying. He was a mess. I found out later he was doing heroin again. He wanted to get back together and wrote me a letter. I was no longer attracted to him and it broke his heart. I was trying to do better, and he was still doing a lot of damaging things.

On July 5th, 2001, I got the call that he had died. His brother said he passed away from hepatitis and cirrhosis of the liver. He was only 32 years old. I was working at Home Depot at the time and cleaning houses on the side. We went to the funeral and Mark took it hard. He looked horrible—swollen and bloated. I remember Mark telling me he couldn't believe he wasn't ever going to see him again. This was the first death Mark had experienced.

I continued to work for Home Depot for a few more months. I was a lot tech, the first female lot tech they ever had. That meant I pushed carts and loaded cars. I enjoyed it and was made employee of the month shortly after starting. I was in the break room on September 11, 2001, when the news showed the first plane had hit the tower. We all stood there in shock as we watched the second plane hit. I left to go pick up my kids from school. Everyone thought we were going to war. Dawn thought I was there to get her out early because it was her birthday.

I quit my job at Home Depot and ramped up my cleaning business. It had been a rough few years of loss. A year and half earlier while living in the motel, I got the call that Johnny had overdosed on heroin and died. Terri had been with him, and she said he did the shot and fell to his knees, turned gray and died. She just left him there. She took the drugs and left. I don't think she even called the ambulance. My two long-time loves were now gone forever.

I was haunted about where they were now. I thought they must be in hell. It was tormenting me. I was still here for a reason and I knew it. That was pretty much the end of relationships for me. I had put men and drinking and drugs before my kids for years so, now I made up my mind that things were going to be different. It was critical for me to spend more time with my kids while they were teenagers. I was only 39 with two teens depending on me as their provider, but I was still really immature.

I was keeping the promise that I made to Mark. He was doing well at Bordentown High School. He had actually made some really good friends and would bring them over to the house sometimes. One day, I was laying on the couch when they all walked in high as a kite. They were giggling and tried to get to his room as fast as possible. What could I say? They grew up with a mom who partied all the time. I never smoked weed in front of them, but they saw me buzzed from drinking for many years.

I had actually stopped smoking weed for many years because it made me think too much, then I would get paranoid. As I got older, I just stuck to drinking just beer. I had left the hard liquor alone after my 20s. My 20s were a blur because I drank rum and coke all the time. That hard liquor would cause me to black out. Now that I was getting older and had a little more self-control, I said little because I was still addicted to Xanax, which I had been doing for almost 19 years at this point. It became a standard in my life, and I felt that I needed it.

As my cleaning business grew, we managed to have eleven houses to clean. This business was not only our lively good, but it's something that Dawn and I did together. With all the time we spent together cleaning houses, we were able to get really close. We would hang out all the time laughing and thrift shopping. I was thankful for this time with my daughter and thankful for the bond that we had developed. It was nothing like the relationship I had with my parents when I was her age. I began to realize that a cycle was broken, and I knew deep in my heart that I truly cherished my kids, all of them, even my son that lived with my parents.

That old car of mine lasted a year before it completely died in front of a store in Trenton. Thankfully, it was tax time again, and I went to a car dealer and got a white Ford Contour. This was a better-looking car and not as old as the Chrysler. Transportation was key to Dawn and me to operate our business.

Dawn had met her first real best friend at Eagle Rock. Her name was Gabby and she was beautiful. When Dawn wasn't with me, she was with Gabby. We had it pretty good there. Mark would have his friends over and as terrible as it is, I would let them smoke and drink. I guess my immaturity played a part in that, but I wanted to know that they were in a safe environment where I could watch over them. With my history of being addicted to one thing or another from the time I was 11, I understood in my own way. I put my kids through a lot and they just mimicked what they saw me do. So if they were home, I felt better than having them have to live through some of the bad situations I often put myself through. I'm not sure if I was right or wrong, but this is how I felt and this is what I had done.

Mark dated a few girls, but then he met a girl a few years older than him. The first time she came to my house she walked in without knocking. Her name was Tina, and we didn't really like each other. She was head strong and so was I. He was 17 when he got her pregnant. I let her move in with us for a while, but it didn't last. Her grandmother owned property, and they ended up moving out into a house in Trenton. He was almost 18 and graduated, so I gave him my blessing and let him go.

One night when Dawn was 14, she stayed out all night. I woke up and realized she hadn't come home. I panicked. I eventually found out she was with an older guy, Alex; he had just turned 18. I called his mother and threatened to press charges on him. He was Puerto Rican. When I got her home, I had to explain to her what happened to me when I was young—how I was abducted and taken all over the country. She was shocked and started crying. She never stayed out all night again. I knew that she was still seeing him because she was head over heels for him. So, eventually I changed my mind and allowed her to date him. He lived in the hood in Trenton. He was really good looking with beautiful green eyes. I used to go pick him up and let him hang out at our house. Dawn had grown up fast due to the lifestyle I lived, moving her and Mark all over creation. I got along great with Alex. Our birthdays were a day apart in August. He was young and ran around with his friends all the time. There were things I saw him do that I did not like because I knew she deserved better. There would be times when Dawn would be all dressed up waiting for him to show up, and he would never show. I also saw some traits in him that I did not like; for example, he was jealous and controlling over her. Even though Alex and I learned to get along, I still had concerns for my daughter.

Dawn was almost 16 by the time we moved again. Tina told me her grandmother had a small apartment for rent across the street from where she and Mark were living. Dawn was still seeing Alex, and we were still cleaning houses. I figured paying $500 in rent was better than $800 in rent, so we moved. It was a cute one-bedroom place with an attic. I took the living room and gave Dawn the bedroom. I washed down the walls several times because whoever lived there before me was a smoker. We fixed it up real nice and settled in. My first grandson was born July 7th, 2003. They named him Xander, and he was beautiful. I got to take him every other weekend. He was an easy baby and a joy to have around. Dawn began hanging out over to Mark's home with Tina a lot and since she was rude to me, I pretty much began to stay to myself. My relationship with Mark began to change. I knew this girl was driving a wedge between us because he started to treat me differently. Her mother had been a crack addict for years, and I guess they were sharing war stories with each other. I could feel tension with Mark, and it was killing me.

I love my son, but I began to realize that he could have

bitter feelings bottled up against me. My lifestyle greatly affected his life over the years. I was doing better now, and no matter how bad it got, I always showed my kids love and never let anyone hurt them.

Brian, on the other hand, had completely stopped talking to me. As he got older, I would call the house to talk to him and every time I was told he wasn't home. It was clear they were trying to keep me away from him. When he turned 17, I received a phone call from him asking me to please sign for him to get his driver's license. I immediately jumped in the car and met him at the DMV. I received a letter from him asking if he could stay with me because my parents didn't want him to go to college. I was so excited and I wrote back telling him yes. In the letter, I shared that I would rent a bigger house if he came so that he could be with me. I don't think my parents ever gave him the letter because he never talked to me again. He rejected me from that point on. I think it may have been because he wanted to join the Secret Service, and they do extensive background checks on your family. I'm sure my father filled him in on all my past sins and who his father was. I tried to reach out to him but he rejected me at every turn. I can't say I blame him, but it was just so painful, so I stopped trying.

So here I was up in this apartment alone most of the time thinking about everything I had been through and all the loss in my life. I began watching the show *Crossing Over with John Edward,* where he would contact the dead relatives of people. I thought I had found the answer to life after death. I still was not aware of what the Bible said about these things. I was just trying to figure out where Tammy, Johnny, and George were spending eternity. We began going to physics, and I began visiting graveyards trying to catch ghosts on video.

During this time, I was still doing cough syrup and I was sinking into a depression. I had my apartment decorated with black curtains and darkness. I had a tarantula spider as a pet. I set up the attic like a tomb. I had black and white pictures of graves hanging on the wall. I had an old wheelchair up there, I had candles and scary music playing. I don't know what I was thinking, but I now realize why I was in the state of depression I was in. I had isolated myself in darkness. I was searching for answers and I was looking in all the wrong places.

Dawn had been kicked out of school for tapping dirt off her shoe into a teacher's coffee cup. They had a zero-tolerance policy after the act of terrorism on the Twin Towers. She had a tutor for a while and then was sent to an alternative school in Burlington. It was a school for bad kids. Eventually, she stopped going all together. We had met a lady named Maria, and Dawn used to babysit for her. We had been warned by a psychic to stay away from Maria.

One night I had what I now call a prophetic dream. Dawn and I were in a small closed park, and it was surrounded by a gate. There was a group of Puerto Rican girls in the park, and they were after Dawn. They were dressed in short skirts and had no underwear on. They were swinging on the swing with open legs and laughing. Bats were flying all around, and snakes were slithering on the ground. One of the girls picked up a snake and bit it. Her teeth came through the other side. They had knives, and I was trying to get Dawn away from them. It switched to me hitchhiking down the highway holding an aborted baby. It was a baby that Terri's niece had aborted, and I was frantically trying to get it help, I was breathing in the baby's mouth and it was horrific. I woke up in a cold sweat, and immediately felt like my daughter was in danger. I warned her after telling her the dream to be careful that I had a feeling someone wanted to hurt her. This was late August of 2004. We had been living in the apartment for about a year. Dawn would be turning 17 in a month, and I had little control over her at this point. One night she went to go babysit for Maria, and I couldn't shake the feeling that she was in danger.

It was close to Alex's birthday, and they were supposed to be going to Atlantic City to get a room with another couple. Alex waited too long to let Dawn know, so she decided to babysit for Maria and make some money. I had tried to call her several times, and she didn't answer. Alex called, and I told him she was over there babysitting. I told him to have her call me as soon as he saw her. I was literally shaking. When she finally called, I was relieved and I told her to be careful that I had a bad feeling. That was a Friday night. She came home and spent the next two days with me. She got a phone call from Alex's brother telling her to take Alex and leave town. He told her that the girl Alex was renting a basement from was murdered, and they were coming for him. Dawn broke down crying and confessed to me that Alex was in a gang. He had started a war between two gangs when he left one and joined another. I couldn't believe she kept this from me for three years.

With all the street smarts I had, I had absolutely no clue this kid was in a gang. Now all the feelings I had started to make sense. About an hour later, we got a phone call from Alex saying he was in the hospital but didn't know what happened or how he got there. He said his eyes were burning and his neck hurt. He also said there were guards on his door. He didn't know yet that his roommate was dead. She was a Latin Queen in the gang and a mother of two young girls. They had taken her down to the basement and tried to shoot her in the head. The gun jammed, and they went out and got another one and executed her. The next morning a neighbor saw the girls outside playing alone and asked them where Mommy was. They told the neighbor Mommy was a monster mommy. The cops were called, and they found her body in the basement.

We went to see Alex in the hospital, and it was heartbreaking. His eyes were completely red; every blood vessel was burst. He had bloody choke marks around his neck several times. We started crying when we saw him. He had grown up in the hood and joined the Neta's street gang at a young age. A few months before this incident, he was jumped by a rival gang and was stabbed in the back with a broken beer bottle. His gang didn't help him, and it left a bad taste in his mouth. He ended up leaving the Neta's and joining the Latin Kings. It stirred up a bunch of trouble between the gangs, and after he and his brother were beat down by the Neta's, a hit was put out on him.

On the night they were supposed to go to Atlantic City, fellow gang members dropped him off at Maria's to be with Dawn. He introduced Dawn to them, and they seemed really pissed that they weren't going to Atlantic City. The girl gave Dawn a look. During their relationship, Alex had kept her sheltered from gang life. We were thinking that they probably planned to do the hit that night in Atlantic City, but Dawn spoiled the plans. The psychic had told Dawn to stay away from Maria. If she had stayed away, she would have been going with them that night. I was completely shaken up with the bad feelings that night, not to mention my dream.

That Sunday the old gang beat him down, and the Latin Kings walked away. He went back to his roommate's house, and the gang took him for a ride. He was in the front seat, and someone in the backseat wrapped a wire around his throat and choked him out. They drove him to a place called Duck Island, took off his clothes, and tossed him in a dumpster. They thought he was dead, but he survived. The gang went back to tie up loose ends and kill his roommate because she saw them all leave together. Alex climbed out of the dumpster, and the State Troopers found him disoriented walking down 295 in his boxers. He was looking on the ground saying snakes were trying to get him. I knew at that point the dream I had was a warning from God. He knew I was searching for answers and looking for peace and he let me know it was time to flee the darkness I had embraced.

The gang unit wanted to question Alex because they were starting the investigation. I told Alex's mother that I would take him to Florida. We knew he was in danger, and she was happy to hear that I was willing to take him. Alex was a complete basket case. He suffered memory loss from the attack. When the police were done questioning him and he was released from the hospital, I took him and Dawn to Cinnaminson and put them in the Northern Motor Lodge. I would go back and forth every few days and pack up and have yard sales to get as much money together as possible. I would be sitting on my porch selling my stuff, and the gang members would drive by and give me dirty looks. It took me two weeks to get everything in order.

Tina stopped allowing us to get Xander, and Mark had underlying issues with me so it was a little easier to leave. I had to keep my daughter safe and I didn't want Alex killed. It was hard for me to keep Alex calm and occupied in the room. He was clearly suffering from PTSD, and he was confused a lot. Dawn turned 17 September 11th, and we went to Terri's house to have a small party. We were drinking and Alex was acting crazy in front of my friends. We tried to sleep for a few hours, but Dawn and Alex were arguing. We left to go back to the room, and Alex took his knife and cut his hand open in my car. I was done trying to help him. I kicked him out of my car, and Dawn and I left for Florida the next day.

Even though I traveled to Florida several times, I was nervous driving that far. We didn't have GPS, but we did have a map printed out for us to follow. We also had our cat Levy with us. I think I only drove six hours before we stopped and got a room. Before we hit the highway, I stopped at my parents' house and made peace with them. I told them I was sorry for being such a troubled teenager, and I forgave them for anything I was holding against them. I was leaving a bunch of garbage behind and looking forward to a fresh start with my daughter. God was giving us signs the entire trip. We were finding gospel tracks and running into Christians.

We stopped in Orlando, and it was completely different

from when we used to live there. It was drug-infested, and we only spent one night there in a room. I remembered how nice Ft. Lauderdale was, and we decided we might as well move near the beach. We were so excited when we pulled up to a place right across from the ocean. We rented an efficiency room for $310 a week. We had enough money to keep the place for a few months while we looked for jobs. They used to block the street off every Friday and have block parties. We would go out drinking and dancing. It was so nice down there, and we were enjoying ourselves.

We were finally about to find work cleaning a big office building at night. We had the keys and worked at our own pace. We were able to continue to stay at our beachfront efficiency. We were there for about three months when Mark flew down with his friend for a visit. I was happy to see him. We found a cheaper apartment away from the beach for $600 a month. We used to drive down to South Beach and hang out on Friday night. One night I went out to a bar alone because Dawn couldn't get in. I was sitting by myself and the place was full. Nobody was talking to me and I felt so alone. I thought about Dawn being home alone and I left. I was starting to realize that this party life was useless and empty.

When we had lived by the beach, two women had moved into the place next to us. They were from Texas. One of them looked like she was pregnant, but it was actually a big tumor. They came to seek a natural doctor to treat her cancer. One day she was in a lot of pain, so I went to lay hands on her and pray for her. I wasn't living right, but I knew prayer worked. As I prayed for her, she cried out loud that she was being punished for having a late term abortion. She killed her baby because her boyfriend didn't want it. She was life flighted home and passed away. I began thinking about my own mortality.

I was thinking about everything that had been going on in my life. God was working on me and He was about to reveal himself to me in a big way. It was Christmas 2004, and I was drinking wine on an empty stomach all day. I was cutting up pictures and gluing them to a giant picture frame. I had them separated in order by years. My teen years, my 20s, then my 30s. I was drunk by the time I was done with it. I laid down on the couch and looked at it hanging on the wall. I was disgusted at what I was looking at. Most of the people in the photos were dead and I was either drunk or high in every picture. It was 25 years of a wasted life with a long string of dead friends in the wake. The room started spinning and I yelled to Dawn to help me. I needed to puke. She came and held my hair back as I cried out to Jesus, repenting and begging him to forgive me. I had reached the end of myself and my need for a savor was never so clear.

The next day I just wanted to find a church. We drove around, but couldn't find one open. I was done with drinking. Our neighbors had offered us drinks on New Year's, but I declined. That Wednesday was January 5, 2005, Dawn and I drove across town to Calvary Chapel in Ft. Lauderdale. That Wednesday evening, I rededicated my life to Christ and Dawn got saved. It felt like a weight was lifted off me. We had a small little T.V. and the only station we could get clear was TBN. I watched it constantly. The church gave us bibles and we began to read the word. I was like a sponge and God was downloading so much information into my spirit. I felt like I could explode. Every time I thought of a question someone on T.V would teach on the subject. I trusted God and poured my Xanax down the toilet. I had no serious withdrawal and I had taken them for 20 years. I went on a 3 day fast. I had never been discipled the right way. I would try to stay on the right path over the years, but was still filling my spirit with garbage music and movies. I got rid of all my cds and movies. Passion of the Christ came out and I saw what Jesus had done for me. I couldn't get enough of God. I was up at night and I was praying for the little four unit complex we lived in. I was praying for the neighbors to get saved and I could hear screeching spirits flying around the building.

We had our cat Levy and every time Dawn and I tried to read our Bible out loud the cat would run back and forth across the bed and crawl up the curtain. He was full grown not a playful kitten. He was irritated by the word of God. One night he was acting crazy and his eyes were sharp and evil. I cast out whatever was him he puked on the rug and his eyes completely changed back to round and soft.

We were on fire for the Lord and wanted to go out and share the gospel. We purchased some tracks and went to grocery store to tell people about Jesus. We were talking to a homeless lady and at first, she was open to the gospel, but as soon as I led her in prayer and told her to admit she was a sinner, she jumped up cursed me out. She gave us the finger. You could literally see the demon in this woman. A few weeks later we were driving and we saw her. It was like the demon saw us in the car and stared at us as we drove by, it was so eerie.

I was reading the Bible from cover to cover and it took me six months. There were so many things I didn't know. I knew we weren't supposed to have false gods, but I didn't know if they were gods that really existed. I felt like the blinders were off and God was showing me everything. There were times when we ran low and food, but we were so full of joy it didn't bother us. All the old wicked desires had gone away. We were truly new creatures with new desires. Dawn said, "Mom why did I never know about Jesus and what he did for me?" I explained to her that I had never totally surrendered enough to share the truth with her. I tried many times over the years, but it never lasted because I wasn't reading the word of God.

Dawn and I quit working for the cleaning company because the boss was moving us around and having us drive over an hour away to a timeshare building. The people working there treated us poorly and looked down on us, so we quit. Dawn started a job at a dry-cleaning store. She was really missing Alex. He had relocated up north with his cousin to get away from the gangs. She called him, and we allowed him to come to Florida. We wanted to show him how Jesus had changed our lives and wanted him to get saved. I cared about Alex and wanted the best for him. He seemed to like it in Ft. Lauderdale and went to church with us. He accepted Jesus, and we would all do Bible study together.

Dawn left the dry cleaner and started working at 7-Eleven. I answered the phone one day, and it was CVS looking for Dawn about a job. I told them she was working, but I was interested. The store was right around the corner. I was hired immediately. I thought I was being hired as a cashier, but I was put in the photo lab. I was so intimidated and nervous. I had learned the scripture, *I can do all things through Christ who gives me strength,* and I whispered it to myself a lot. Jennifer was the woman training me, and she was patient and soft spoken. She taught me everything I needed to know to run the photo lab. I worked as much as I could, and I never called in sick. Dawn ended up getting hired at the same CVS, and we did a great job for the store. I quickly climbed the ladder and became the photo lab supervisor. Dawn became a shift supervisor. Alex started working next door at Mail Boxes Etc.

He tried his best to stay on the right track, but he became bored and started drinking again. Dawn and I moved out and rented a place on the water by the intercoastal. She was still seeing Alex and eventually ended up pregnant. She gave birth to my second grandson, Eli Xavier on October 14, 2006. He was absolutely beautiful. We were able to adjust our schedules at work to accommodate the baby. I worked days and she worked nights. I was doing so well at work that I went from making $7.50 an hour to making $13 an hour in three years. I was a fast learner, and CVS was switching over the entire cash register system along with a new digital photo system. I was chosen to be trained and train the rest of the district with the new system. God was taking me places I never thought I would go.

One day Mark called upset and depressed. He was having issues with Tina. He moved down to Florida to be with us. He was a woodworker and found work pretty quickly. His boss liked him, and they would fly to different places to install cabinets and wine racks on boats. I was thrilled that my children had turned so well after everything that was stacked against them. Mark was not interested in the Christian life, but he was a hard worker and I was proud of him.

We all enjoyed Florida together for a while, then Mark

made the decision to travel. Alex moved back up north when Eli was four months old. Dawn and I stayed until August of 2008, and we decided to move to Virginia where my sister Margaret lived. Virginia was nice and we stayed with my sister for a few months. We both got jobs at different CVS stores. We had a blow up with my sister and ended up moving out into our own place. I was only at my job a few months when the ATF did a sting right before Christmas, and I was fired for selling cigarettes to a minor.

Discouraged, things began to take a sour turn. Dawn and I began slipping in our walk with the Lord. That spring we were hanging out with the neighbors and started drinking and smoking weed. Dawn began dating a guy, and it wasn't long before she was pregnant with her second child. I was devastated, and it was a hard pill to swallow. Eli was almost three, and Dawn and I had been planning to move to Hawaii. We could feel the winds of change, and it seemed as if it was always around September that our lives would go through a change.

Dawn didn't want to leave the guy she was seeing, but she chose to stick with our plan. We sold everything we owned and boarded a Greyhound Bus headed to Los Angeles. As soon as I got on that bus, I knew I was making a big mistake. We thought if we got to California, it would be cheaper to fly over to Hawaii. Unfortunately, that was not the case. We stepped off the bus in downtown L.A. after three days of a long, grueling bus trip. I was shaking and did not know what was wrong with me. I knew this was not God's will for us.

We had to get out of that part of town as soon as possible. We hailed a cab, and he took us to a decent hotel. Rooms were $100 a night. The cab driver stole our most important bag with everything we needed to shower and Dawn's contact lenses. I soon found out tickets were just as much, and it wasn't going to happen. There was a reason we didn't make it to Hawaii in 2009 and that would be revealed later. We ended up staying in California for two weeks and ran through all our money before boarding the next bus back to Virginia. Another three-day trip back to Virginia.

My sister and I had made peace, and she allowed us to come back to her house. We spent the next few months at Margaret's house, and it was fun. We laughed a lot, and Dawn was moving along in her pregnancy. My sister had a Franklin Stove and we would huddle in the living room and watch movies. I ended up getting hired at Walmart. Dawn went to the OB doctor to find out the sex of her baby, and we were informed that the baby was a girl, and she had a hole in her heart. We were trusting God and praying for healing. As the pregnancy progressed, the issue became more serious.

We made many trips back and forth from Charlottesville,

Virginia to UVA University Hospital for ultrasounds. Dawn was six months pregnant and named her baby Ava. The doctors tried more than once to convince her to abort her baby. We were horrified. This baby had a name, and we trusted God to pull her through. Dawn ended up getting a nice amount of taxes and unemployment at the same time, and we were able to rent a really nice remodeled home a few blocks from Margaret. It had 3 bedrooms and a full basement with a large backyard. We went shopping and bought a lot of new things for the place. We were content and very comfortable.

Mark had been traveling all over the country, and he came to visit. He was sleeping on the couch and told us he felt like something was wrong. He said the cat was going crazy at night running up and down the basement stairs. I began to do some research after I went through a serious bout of depression. I had no reason to be depressed. Things were going great and I was working. One day while talking to the neighbor across the street she asked me if I knew what happened in the house. Apparently, the last tenant was a long-distance truck driver who had a girlfriend he left behind while he traveled. She cheated on him and he did not take it well. One day he came home and hastily parked his truck and went inside. When he didn't come back out, neighbors grew concerned. They found him hanging from the staircase in the basement. I got the full story from the landlord when I asked him about it. He had cut his wrists first and was soaking his arms in a bucket of water. When that failed, he went down and hung himself. Now I understood why I was feeling so much oppression in the home. We ended up anointing the doors and windows and told whatever was hanging around the house to leave in Jesus' name.

Chapter 9

The Devil is a Liar

Dawn was due in April, and they wanted to induce labor and have a team of heart specialists ready immediately after birth in case of complications. We drove to UVA on April 8th of 2010 for her to be admitted. My sister and niece followed us up there for support. Ava Lilliana Rose Keane was born the next afternoon. She was very swollen, and they whisked her away to run tests to see how bad her condition was and see what the next move would be. We were believing for healing.

We were devastated when they informed us that she would need open heart surgery. We were getting ready to face another battle, and we put our trust in God. Dawn was vigilant at learning everything she needed to know about the care of Ava. Tests revealed that she had a congenital heart defect, Truncus Arteriosus. Genetic testing also showed that it was due to the fact that she had a condition called DiGeorge syndrome or Q22.11 deletion. She was missing a part of the 22nd chromosome. They informed us of what that meant. She would have some learning disabilities and possible behavior problems. We just stood on God's word and rebuked any curses they were speaking.

We were becoming very frustrated with the lack of care she was receiving. They had shaved her head in a bowl cut with a dry razor. They were trying to place a picc line but were unsuccessful. Dawn was devastated when she saw what they did to her hair. They placed the picc line in her leg, and we noticed it becoming red and swollen. When we brought it to the attention of the nurses, we were ignored and written off. It ended up getting infected, and she was put on antibiotics for two weeks. That pushed back her surgery. When she finally had surgery, we could tell the doctor was holding something back from us. Ava was having a hard time breathing, and we could not get her off the vent. They finally came clean and informed us that they nicked her diaphragm, and she would need another surgery to fix the issue. We were staying at the Ronald McDonald house. Because we lived an hour and a half away, Dawn could be at the hospital with Ava. I would take care of Eli while she tended to Ava.

Dawn was under tremendous stress, and she was pumping breast milk for Ava. She couldn't feed by mouth, so they were feeding her through a tube in her nose. Dawn had been keeping a notebook of everything that went on with Ava's care. The nurses were careless and would change her diaper than mess around with her IV that went directly to her heart. We did not stay silent. We went in one day, and Ava had poop going all the way up her back. We had been taking photos all along. We had pictures of her leg that had been infected. After many different incidents, I called patient relations and demanded a meeting. I printed out all the photos, and we had an entire table full of staff at the meeting. Other parents were complaining as well, and we informed them we were getting ready to contact the newspaper. They stepped up care after that and handed out surveys to everyone for feedback.

One day Dawn was extremely stressed out. She was constantly pumping, and it took all her nutrients out. She passed out in the hospital. The stress was taking a toll on her. Ava wasn't feeding well, but we knew why. They were pushing her feeds into the tube so fast that she was puking everything back up. One night the vent tube came out of her mouth, and her stats dropped immediately. They actually picked it up off the floor and shoved it down her throat so hard they damaged her vocal cord. You couldn't even hear her cry. It was a nightmare. Dawn was the youngest mom in there, and she was the best mom as far as speaking up about the care she expected.

She knew what all the numbers were supposed to be

because she researched all the medications. We were desperate to go home, but until Ava could get off the vent and eat a certain amount, we were stuck there. We finally got her breathing on her own, but eating took longer. They wanted to place a G tube in her belly for feeding but after we researched it and prayed about it, we decided against it. Dawn insisted they let her bottle feed, and she began to keep her food down because she was drinking at a slow pace. After three very frustrating months, we finally got to take Ava home. She was released July 9th. We still had to supplement her feed by tube feeding her in the nose. They taught us both how to do it. We were also given a home nurse to help overnight.

We were thrilled to finally get her home into her own crib. The medical supplies were delivered, and we met with the nurse. Her name was Angel, and we got along with her very well. She took care of Ava through the night. The doctors were telling us Ava would be with the nose feeding for six months or more, after about a month, she pulled out the tube. We just worked consistently with her, and she didn't need the tube or nurse any longer.

The next battle was right around the corner, and this blow would test our faith like never before. It was again the end of August about six weeks after getting Ava home. Dawn came out of the bathroom and told me she felt like something was blocking her vaginal opening. We got a mirror, and you could see something was not right. We called the ambulance, and they transported her to Lynchburg General Hospital. They thought it was a fibroid. It turned out to be a tumor the size of a softball. She was scheduled to have it removed that Friday. The kids and I waited in the hospital all day as she underwent surgery. The doctor informed me they were sending it off to be tested and set Dawn up for an appointment to see the oncologist. As we sat in the office of Michael Douvas at UVA, we were puzzled because we never got confirmation from the hospital if the tumor was cancer. Tears streamed down my face as we got the devastating news that she had a rare and aggressive form of cancer called small cell carcinoma. This type of cancer usually was found in the lungs, but it had attached itself to her cervix. We saw the OB-GYN Oncologist next, and it was a grim diagnosis. Dawn did her best to comfort me and tell me everything would be ok. I couldn't believe we had just gotten Ava on track and now this. They told us because she was a young mother, they were going to fight this with everything they could. She was scheduled to start chemo in two weeks. When she was done, she would have a radical hysterectomy removing everything including her ovaries. It would immediately send her into menopause. The last treatment would be radiation. We did our best to prepare for the battle.

Dawn had always been a positive girl, she would encourage me over the years. We thought it was possible that she had been so stressed out caring and worrying about Ava that it opened a door for this vile disease. She kept her chin up as we began this next chapter of our lives. I had quit my job at Walmart after Ava was born and I couldn't go back to work now as I would become my daughter's caregiver.

My sister Margaret was a big support system for us, and she did everything in her power to help us through this difficult process. Dawn had long, beautiful, curly hair, and it was heartbreaking knowing it was going to fall out. Margaret took us to have family pictures done after her first treatment. She paid for her to get a cute haircut before she lost her hair. Mark came back for a visit and went with her for her next treatment. Her hair was thinning, and I tried to fight back tears when he stood in the bathroom with her shaving her head completely. The cancer center was great and had programs in place for wigs and beauty items to try and help the self-esteem of the women fighting this wretched sickness. I never heard her gripe or complain. She never said why me. I was thinking how awful it would be if I lost my beautiful daughter. We had endured so much together. I thought back to when I was pregnant with her so many years earlier. How I didn't want to be pregnant and how it was so hard for me to bond with her as an infant. God never makes mistakes when He sends a soul to be born. He knew the end from the beginning and gave me a daughter that was strong and beautiful, caring, and giving—someone to grow with and learn new things with.

We experienced the love of Christ together, and she was my absolute best friend. The thought of losing her was heart wrenching, and I tried not to go there.

I faced many difficulties over the years, but watching my daughter suffer through cancer was one of the hardest things I went through. We moved her bed into the living room, so we could be together as much as possible and I could tend to her needs. We went through some financial problems, but people helped us get through. Our landlord gave us a free month's rent, and the neighbors dropped off cards from church members with cash to help with bills. I was always good at figuring out how to make a way to get by. We began to sell items to make ends meet on Craigslist.

Dawn was completely bald and losing weight. She had always been very concerned about her appearance, making sure she always looked her best when going out. Her hair was beautiful and always had her nails done. This trial she endured with cancer totally broke her down to the bare bones and caused her to be completely humbled. We both had faith going through the battle, but we weren't living totally surrendered to the Lord. We were both self - medicating while going through this.

It was during this time that the family from New Jersey started calling. Sometimes it takes a serious illness for family to reach out. I found out my father made a comment that if Dawn passed away, they wouldn't be able to travel for a funeral. I would have never expected that anyway. She did pretty well during the chemo. She got sick, but she never complained. The worst part of everything was when she went to have the hysterectomy. It was supposed to be a three-hour surgery, and she was in the operating room for eleven hours before I got to finally see her. She looked horrible and was in agony. I felt helpless. There was nothing I could do to take her pain away. When I got her home, she was still suffering. She would be sitting on the toilet screaming in pain. I would call the doctor telling them she needed stronger medication.

Back and forth, we drove to UVA. It was a nightmare. Next step was radiation, and she seemed to handle that pretty well. It was an ordeal that took about a year and a half before she was done with everything. We would go for scans every six months and go to Ava's heart appointments. It was a whirlwind of a couple years with constant medical issues. Ava was facing procedures as she grew with the heart. She would need to have stents placed to open up the blood flow. They told us she would most likely need two more open heart surgeries as she grew. They had placed a pig valve in her heart, and it would not grow as she did. She had speech delay, and a therapist came to the house and worked with her. She taught her how to sign a few words.

By the spring of 2012, we were beginning to see the light

at the end of the tunnel. Ava was thriving and Dawn was gaining weight; her hair was growing back. We really learned a lot of lessons through everything we went through. We were so close and appreciated everything we had, especially each other. We saw how precious the gift of life was and how quickly things can change. We didn't feel like God was punishing us for backsliding, but we were aware when we weren't living in His will. We learned that if you allow certain things in your life, you can leave the door open for the enemy. We knew God was trying to get our attention again. There is just no denying the truth; when you have lived with the goodness of the Lord and turn away, it is exactly how the Bible describes—like a dog returning to its vomit. We were grateful He spared our family after such serious illnesses, and we were ready to get back on track with the Lord. Dawn made the first move in the right direction. She began to seek him again, read her word, and stopped doing the things that didn't please Him. It took me about another month, but by late fall of 2012, we both surrendered. He was pouring into us like never before. It was as if He was taking us to the next level. Dawn would be sitting on the couch reading the word of God, and she would feel hot oil in her belly as He revealed spiritual truth to her. It was beautiful.

Chapter 10

More Loss

In May of 2012, my brother Eddie tried to commit suicide. He was the oldest son that did everything right in my father's eyes. I was the black sheep, and Eddie and I hadn't spoken in over 25 years. My sisters were on the outs with him and really had nothing nice to say about him. I never hated any of my family members except my dad when I was younger, but God had really softened my heart over the years. I desperately wanted to contact my brother. I wrote him a letter and asked him to forgive me for being an embarrassment of a sister when we were young. I told him I forgave him and I loved him. I shared how Jesus had saved me and completely changed my life. I told him he survived for a reason, and that hell was real. I gave him my phone number and was thrilled when I received a text from him. He called me Bernie. He said how happy he was to get my letter and that he loved me. He told me to tell my sisters he loved them. None of them were talking at the time, and

I was so excited that God was using me to be a peacemaker.

I told my sisters, and they reconciled with him. He began to send me text messages from time to time. He was extremely depressed and was drinking while taking Xanax and antidepressants. He was separated from his wife and was alone in a big house. One day I was on the treadmill and feeling great about our lives. I was losing weight and feeling good. My girls were alive and thriving. I looked at Dawn and said things are going great for us right now, I'm actually content. The phone rang 30 minutes later, and it was my niece telling me my brother Eddie committed suicide. I fell to my knees and cried out to God asking why. I was willing to lead him to the Lord. I just needed more time. Immediately, I thought of my brother in hell. It was tormenting me constantly. I would think of him being thirsty, if I sat outside on a nice day with warm breezes. I thought how awful it was that he would never experience that simple pleasure again.

He left behind two beautiful daughters, and they were the ones that found him. My niece was pregnant with his first grandchild. They went over to clean the house for him and found him dead in a chair with a bag over his head. He ordered some sickening suicide kit off the internet. He purchased a tank of helium from a party store and inhaled it till he died. It was absolutely devastating for our family. My father had the nerve to try to have us not come up for the funeral. I spoke to my niece, and she reassured me that we were more than welcome to come. This was the first sibling I lost, and I wanted to go. We traveled to New Jersey with my sister Margaret and stayed at my best friend's house the first night. Bobby D was someone I trusted, and he made us feel right at home during this difficult time. The funeral was horrible and very heart-wrenching. It was so hard seeing the pain of his two daughters and even seeing that my parents were completely broken. My son, Brian was now a police officer near Atlantic City, and he was there in uniform. I don't know why he wore that, but he looked at me with a proud and haughty look of disgust. I didn't understand why he would act like that towards me at a funeral. I was already in enough pain, and that just broke my heart more. My brother had left letters to certain people, and he mentioned me in his letter. H had been happy I reached out to him.

It wasn't until a few years after his death that I found out he had instructed his wife to give us a decent amount of money for Ava. It hurt me more than anything. It wasn't the money that mattered. It was that I was never told. Death does things to a family that I will never understand. His wife and daughters were blaming my parents for his death; my sisters were blaming his wife. They were all being ugly, and I wanted no part of it. You would think death would be an eye opener and force families to treat each other better. It's a sad state of affairs when hatred and accusations are thrown around. I didn't feed into any of it.

My father didn't learn from his death, either. He ended up having issues with my younger brother and they stopped talking. My father is a very strict Catholic. It just reinforced my beliefs that the Catholic religion means nothing. Here he is going to church every week and harboring unforgiveness in his heart for my brother. After Eddie died, he was going to see the priest a lot. He claimed the priest told him the church had changed their minds about suicide sending people to hell. I don't know if my brother cried out to God for forgiveness before he died. I pray he did. I couldn't help thinking he ended up in hell like my husband and the other people who passed away in my life. I knew what God's word said that without Christ, you don't inherit the kingdom of God. I know the road is narrow and few find it. I also knew that it didn't matter how many times my dad went to church and gave the priest money. If he died with unforgiveness in his heart, he would not make it to heaven. The Lord's Prayer says for us to forgive those who trespass against us. I don't want anyone to go to hell.

My parents are now in their 80s, and I don't call or talk to them much because it's uncomfortable. I pray that the Lord will use me to bring them to the truth of the gospel. I was completely rejected by them because I accepted Christ all those years ago. I made a deal with God that if He has my father call me, I will tell him about the real Jesus and how we must forgive. They never call so if he does, I know it will be because God thinks I am ready to put my fears aside and speak truth. I have friends who have had death in the family cause division and strife, mostly over money. I guess for me I was satisfied with having just enough to get by because I knew what it was like to struggle and have nothing. I didn't have help when I was living in motels and homeless shelters. I was just glad my kids were with me. I don't care if I get anything from anyone when they pass away. My father told me years ago that he spoke to his lawyer when preparing his will, and he left me one dollar. I'm actually glad I was poor and if I wanted something I worked for it. I know the word of God says store up your treasures in heaven. My sisters have been married to men that helped take care of them and provided a decent lifestyle for them. I never had that because I was dealing with drug addicts and alcoholics. I know that my family has been affected by the curse of depression. It does not matter how much money or possessions you acquire. If you don't have peace in your heart, you don't have anything.

Over the years, my family has accused us of being in a cult because of the things we believe. I just continue to pray for them and hope someday they will realize that accepting Christ as Savior is the only way to eternal life. Alcoholism runs in our family as well. I never thought I would be able to stop drinking, but with Christ all things are possible. I believe that most families have generational curses, and they have to be broken by the blood of Jesus. My grandmother suffered from depression. Everyone in my family has struggled with it at different times. When I was younger and before Christ, I was constantly depressed. He came to set the captives free, and I rarely have to deal with it anymore. The only time it rears its ugly head is when I am allowing things into my life that need not to be there. We fight those things by staying in His word and praying. I hope that if my family reads this book one day, they will realize that the only hope we have for some kind of peace here on earth is only found when we surrender everything to Christ. We cannot claim to be Christians and still live like the world. Christ said it Himself if we are lukewarm, He will spew us out of His mouth. We cannot live for the devil and expect to reach the Kingdom when we die.

Dawn and I were smart and knew how to get things done. We were a great team, and we just moved forward and stronger in the Lord. We did deep dives into the Word and asked Him to reveal the truth to us. We had always believed in pre-trib rapture, but God was showing us in His word that was not the case. Matthew 24 was clear about what would take place. Jesus said we would be hated for His name's sake, and we would be led away in chains and killed because of Him. He was showing us how all the holidays that we celebrated had pagan roots and did not honor Him in any way. The pagans would cut down the tree and decorate it with silver. Jesus never told us to celebrate His birthday. He wasn't even born in December. Easter was also pagan. The dying of eggs and the bunny all had roots from wicked practices. Halloween was the worst. The church would still have trick or trunk and decorate the cars with spooky webs and dark images. God's word showed us that light should have nothing to do with darkness. The Satan worshippers will tell you Halloween was their holy day when they sacrificed the kids that had been snatched the few months before. You'll notice in September and the beginning of October missing children increase; that's not a coincidence. We stopped celebrating all of them. If anything, we should be observing the Jewish Holy Days. They were the ones Jesus took part in because he was Jewish. The Bible says seek and you shall find, and the more seeking we did, the more God was revealing. He was leading us to people who had shows on YouTube that had knowledge of the deep things of God.

One day I was looking up aliens and came across a video of a guy named Steve Quayle. He was teaching about Genesis 6 and the giants. Everything was backed up from scripture. The Bible was more interesting than I thought. We started listening to a show called Hagmann and Hagmann. It was a father and son team who were Christians and had guests who taught on different subjects. We learned about the deep state and evil doings of the government. It was like another awakening; scales had fallen off our eyes. Some people would say we were conspiracy theorists, but I call us conspiracy realists. It all made sense. It was a spiritual battle between good and evil.

Our eyes were opened to all the shows we allowed the kids to watch. Disney is full of witchcraft and spells. It taught magic and the princess syndrome of stuck up and pampered little girls. Pokemon is full of defiant little creatures whose names were demonic and meant rebellion. Everything was packaged so nice, and Christian families were so blind to allow this in the home. We were just as blind, but if you are serious about finding truth, then ask God to reveal it to you; He will. Look how many Christians have all the Harry Potter books and movies in the home and wonder why the kids are having bad dreams. It's witchcraft and spells all geared towards our kids. We went through the entire house and purged everything we felt God did not like. Eli had just received a lot of Batman toys, and when we researched and found the connection to Baphomet, he had no problem giving it up. We dumped out the toy box and collected all the demonic creatures with contorted faces, horns, and weapons. It was like we were seeing the spiritual side of everything. When we were done going through every room, we had two giant garbage bags full of toys, books, knick knacks, and other items ready for a bonfire. We took everything to the back yard and doused it with lighter fluid and set it ablaze. We didn't miss anything. It was gone and the atmosphere in our house began to change. It's a proven fact that spirits can attach themselves to items. Statues of false gods like Buddha should never be in the home of a Christian. Most people have no idea and think its innocent decorations, but certain things can open doors to the demonic.

Chapter 11
New Beginnings

As we began to move forward and put the past few difficult years behind us, we concentrated on our business buying and selling items online. Yard sale pages were just starting to show up on Facebook. We were still selling on Craigslist, but we could reach a lot more people on Facebook. Dawn joined a local group and began posting. They had a lot of stupid rules and kept deleting her posts. I told her we could start our own page. We lived in a small town called Rustburg. We named our page Rustburg Rummage Online Yard sale. Every day we had more and more members joining. That Christmas we made a lot of money selling toys, and we decided that would be our specialty children's items. People were always going to be having babies, so we couldn't lose. We had five Goodwill stores in our area and several other great thrift stores. We would go shopping and completely fill up the van with treasures. We had a big basement and we set up a thrift store. We would hang sale signs every weekend. It seemed like God was giving us great ideas to improve our profits. Our living room became a processing center. We had tons of toys and baby items filling up the dining room. Dawn had a special knack for putting together doll lots. We would purchase toys for .99 cents and sell them for $10 or $15 dollars. These were toys that cost $30 and up in the store. Anyone who has kids knows how expensive toys are. We had a great clientele of repeat customers—lots of grandmothers who wanted a great deal and didn't have time to shop around. It was a win-win for everyone.

We started having online auctions with items we would've sold for $1 at a yard sale. We started the bidding very low at a buck or two and the women would try to outbid each other bringing our profits higher. We could go shopping and buy whatever we wanted. It was wonderful and so much fun. We were working 15 hours a day, staying up till late in the evening posting and filling orders. We would meet up at the Kmart parking lot and literally have a row of cars waiting for us. Dawn would hand out bags as I collected money hand over fist. It was exciting and we loved doing it. We knew it was God pouring out his blessings on us after the enemy had tried his best to destroy our family.

Mark had settled down in Hawaii and came to visit us. He shared his traveling stories and adventures and told us how much he liked living in Hawaii. He was thinking of making it his home. He always came bringing gifts from far away for each of us. On his last visit we discussed possibly moving to Hawaii since it had been our dream to live there some day and our plans in 2009 were thwarted.

After a so-called friend turned us into the tax people, we decided it may be time to relocate. We weren't trying to cheat the system. We just figured they got taxes when someone purchased the item new, taxes again when we purchased the item and we didn't think it was fair they get taxes a third time on the same items. We liquidated everything we owned and purchased four tickets to the big Island in Hawaii. We didn't tell any of our neighbors. We sold almost everything we owned including the cleaning items under the sink. On August 24th, 2015, we had transportation come pick us up and drive us to Richmond for our flight to Hawaii the next day. The kids were excited and so were we. We even got our security deposit back from the landlord; that was a first. I usually ended up owing money. It was definitely time to leave because the neighbors had been treating us weird. They knew we sold stuff from home, and it was as if they looked down on us for it. We didn't care. We were finally getting ready to go live our dream in Paradise. It was a long hard road getting there, but in the end, God gave us the green light to make the move. After a long day of connecting flights, we finally landed on Big Island, and Mark met us at the small Hilo airport.

We arrived in Hilo around 8pm on August 25th, 2015. The humidity hit us like a wall while we went through the tropical airport to retrieve our luggage. We were missing one bag that contained all of Eli's clothing, but were reassured by staff it would be on another flight. My son Mark was waiting for us in a van he borrowed from his friend. We loaded up all the luggage and started the journey 30 minutes up the mountain where Mark was residing in Fern Forest. It was raining and dark when we arrived at his property.

He had built his place 500 feet into the jungle, and we did our best to navigate to the structure he had been working on. His place was pretty open at the time, and the first night was a difficult time for me. The buzzing sound of mosquitoes in my ears was deafening. I covered my head with a blanket and thought I had just made a big mistake leaving the comfort of my Virginia home to come to Hawaii and be hot and uncomfortable. I had become very set in my ways over the five years we lived in our house. This was going to be a major adjustment for me. We did, however, come with enough money to get us started so at least I knew we had options. Mark shares the land with a very nice couple, Tom and Sharon, who were very gracious to us.

We lasted about a week there before I found a two-bedroom house for us to rent. We purchased a car and moved into our new rental. We had an avocado tree outside our kitchen window that had ripe avocado for the picking. We had pineapple plants in the yard, and it wasn't long before we began to get settled. We took daily trips to town trying to learn our way around. It was shocking to see how expensive food prices were. We learned quickly where to shop for the best prices on the things we needed.

There were only two thrift stores on our side of the island, one Goodwill and a Salvation Army thrift store. We had planned to continue our online business, but it was looking like slim pickings for purchasing resell items. The prices were a lot higher than the thrift stores back in Virginia. We went to a few yard sales in the following weeks and realized it would be hard to find decent items this way. A lot of the toys and kid's items were moldy due to the humidity and moisture on the island.

We only sold quality items that were clean and stain free so we were concerned it may not work for us to continue our business. After about a month we managed to find our first decent yard sale and we bought as much stuff possible to get us started. We joined a local yard sale page on Facebook and also started our own group. We were sleeping on airbeds for a while, but little by little we found people leaving the island and purchased some nice beds.

Furniture was hard to come by unless you wanted to pay top dollar. Buying new without neither of us working was not an option, we didn't want to blow through our money too fast. We now had rent to pay and we knew how to search for a bargain so we collected items along the way and made our bedrooms comfortable. Mark would come over and spend the night with us, we would laugh and talk and just hang out spending time together. It was great to have all of us together again. Mark's friend Daveed would come hang out with us, they had been friends for a long time and it was nice to see him again. He was a wealth of knowledge about how to stay healthy and what vitamins food to eat. We enjoyed his company and he was also great at fixing cars, so if I needed something fixed on the car, he would lend hand. We stayed in that house for the first eight months when Mark was given the opportunity to work off the Island for about a year. By this time, he had closed in his house and had windows, walls and screens. He made us the offer to stay there rent-free while he was gone so we could save money to purchase our own land. We decided to take him up on the offer and we moved back up to Fern Forrest. This time was better and we made it very comfortable for ourselves.

We had just gotten a new puppy named Luke, and he moved up the mountain with us. We had rented a storage unit and stored the items we wouldn't need there. Our business was slowly growing. We would schedule our sales when we made trips down the mountain. The days were shorter here, and we had many stops during the day to get everything done. We had to stop at different stores and fill water jugs for drinking and cooking. We were living off grid with limited solar at the time. We collected rainwater for showers. It took some adjusting, but we got used to living this way and began to see how nice it was not having to pay rent or an electric bill. It was absolutely beautiful up in the forest and very peaceful. Neighbors were few and far between and although I was still having second thoughts about moving here. I was beginning to enjoy the beauty and tranquility of the jungle. I did a lot of griping and complaining about the daily grind of going up and down the mountain. The car we purchased was giving us a lot of trouble. It was overheating, and we would have to pull over on the side of the road a lot to let it cool down. I was turning 50 and I was starting to go through menopause. My attitude was poor. I failed to see how blessed I actually was and found myself falling into an angry depression.

Poor Dawn had to put up with me complaining all the time. It was like everything was getting on my nerves. Dawn was homeschooling, and it was irritating for me to hear her struggle to get the kids to cooperate. I hated how long it took us to get done in the stores. I was irked at all the stops we had to make coming up the mountain. As peaceful as it was, I was miserable, and the beginning stages of menopause were taking a toll on my mental state of mind.

We saved up as much money as possible. We found a great deal when we found nine solar panels for $750. They would stay stored on the porch until Mark returned from California. He did return almost a year later with a nice chunk of cash from working hard. He was willing to help us with a loan to purchase our own 3-acre lot. I had decided if we were going to live off grid I wanted to stay up in the Forest. Dawn began looking for a property, and we stayed with Mark for several more months. It was okay, but we were in tight quarters together and we would get on each other's nerves.

There were still some underlying issues between me and Mark. He would make comments about things in the past, and I just knew there were things between us that needed to be dealt with. One day we had a big blow up, and things were said that I was extremely hurt about.

We had purchased a Honda van by this time and I decided to leave his house and stay in the van for a while. I packed up my stuff and took a memory foam mattress and my USB fan and left in the van. I told Dawn to call me if she needed a ride down the mountain. I had no idea where I was going to park the van to sleep, but I quickly learned Walmart parking lot was my best and safest option. I had everything I needed to be comfortable living in the van and it was actually very liberating. It showed me how little I needed in life. I met a few other people that lived out of their vehicles so we watched out for each other. It was probably best for me to experience this because it taught me a new survival skill. I stayed in town in the van for about 3 weeks and then found out Mark was leaving for a trip to the mainland to travel and visit friends and family. I didn't want him to leave without us resolving our issues. If anything happened to him, I would not be able to deal with us not talking. I sent him a message and apologized for not being the best mother when he was younger. We made peace and he left the Island again. I moved back up the mountain with Dawn and the kids. We continued to save more money, so we would have enough to build a structure when we finally found our land.

Mark arrived back on the island a few months later. It took several months to finally find a decent plot of land in the same neighborhood as Mark. This was raw jungle land that needed to be cut in. Mark had experience in clearing land, and I watched Ava and cooked meals while they spent long days clearing the property. Eli went with them and helped. I was surprised how quickly everything was coming together. It was a grueling job for them and most days they worked in the rain. I was still unsure about living off grid, but as I saw the progress they were making, I was really trying to come around to the idea. We hired a guy to come with a D6 and rip through the driveway about 400 feet. It tore through the lava rock and we were well on the way to the next stage. Truckloads of rock were ordered and again they worked long hard days laying rock in the driveway so they would be able to drive Mark's truck down with building supplies. It wasn't long before Mark laid the foundation, and they began building our structure. It took about a month to get the house built, and we were finally able to get over to our property. I'm sure Mark was glad to have his place back to himself. He had been very patient with us living with him in close quarters.

We slowly but surely started settling into our new place. The first winter was very challenging for me because it rained for a month straight. Our house was built about 500 feet back from the road, and we had to carry everything down the long driveway to the house. We would be struggling with umbrellas and mud and I was very irritated with the situation. I continued to gripe and complain and Dawn and I were arguing more and more about everything. I was regretting coming to the island; it was not what I had expected. It was a major adjustment and with me now in full menopause I was miserable, and I was making Dawn miserable right along with me. Mark's friend Daveed ended up moving on the property with us. He was in the front of the property in a large garage type tent from Costco. Dawn and Daveed were spending time together on the property and became close friends. I was irritated and was spending more time by myself contemplating what my options were in case I decided to leave the island. I was actually thinking about moving back to Virginia, but the thought of leaving my grandkids was too painful.

One night Dawn returned home and informed me she had fallen asleep while driving the van up the mountain, and our van was totaled. Now I was stuck up here with no transportation. I would have to rely on others to make trips to town until we were able to get another vehicle. My birthday was approaching and we had the broken-down van on the property. Dawn and Mark took the seats out of the van and set it up for me as a place to get away from the chaos in the house. My nerves were frazzled as Dawn was homeschooling the kids. I just wanted peace and quiet. I enjoyed the van. I had already slept in it when I left Mark's house, so it was not hard for me to make the van my room. I had my comfortable memory foam bed, my fan, my portable DVD player and my phone. I purchased a small cooler to keep some food in. I was comfortable but felt myself slipping into a depression.

My relationship with Dawn had gone downhill and seemed like every time we were together, we ended up getting into an argument. We had both fallen away from God and weren't reading our Bibles. I stayed in the van for about eight months. Dawn had begun talking to a guy we had met when we first moved here. He was attractive, and every time we would run into him at the store or while we were out, I could tell they were attracted to each other. He was friendly and had a great smile. He always complimented her and when we would walk away from seeing him, we would laugh and say how cute he was. He had purchased a few items from us in the past and now they were talking.

Dawn told me they had been chatting online and that he had been going to church and was recently baptized. She had been single for many years and was not looking for a man. I had asked her over the years if she ever wanted to meet a nice guy. She always said that she was satisfied with her life and that her kids were more important. I felt bad sometimes that she didn't ever get to experience having a good relationship with a nice guy. When she told me he had been going to church. I gave her my blessing if she wanted to date him. I had always been so controlling with her, and I was realizing it was time to let her make her own decisions. She had been learning how to run the household on her own since I had been staying in the van. She was learning how to cook and was doing most things by herself. We had always done everything together, but things were changing.

Dawn began dating Ravyn and was spending more time with him at his home down the mountain. I stayed in the house again when she was gone. She was so happy with him and I was happy for her. It wasn't long before she was just staying at his house all the time. He was a single father raising his own two kids, a boy and a girl. They came to me and told me they were thinking about getting married. I thought it was too soon and told them to wait at least a year. They were determined to make a life together and started planning to get married. They were going to church every week and were getting counseling by the pastor. She was meeting women at the church, and the Pastor's wife was very nice to her. I had no skills at preparing for a wedding, so I really didn't do much, but I did help go shopping with her for dresses and clothes for the boys.

They started dating in January, and the wedding was set for April 7, 2019. We were blessed with amazing weather that day, and they got married at Coconut Island in downtown Hilo. I couldn't fight back the tears when my beautiful daughter pulled up and got out of the car in her wedding dress. Ravyn looked handsome. I must admit that they make a beautiful couple. I couldn't have asked for a better son-in-law. He loves my daughter, and he is a hard worker and great provider. His kids are nice and it's just a good fit all around. They had begun the journey of a blended family. I was now an empty nester living completely by myself up the mountain.

I enjoyed my peaceful surroundings, but it wasn't long before I had so much time alone that I began to think a lot. I thought about everything while I was adjusting to living alone. I thought about my childhood and things that had happened to me as a teenager. I thought about the type of mother I had been. I was young and selfish when my kids were growing up, and I had many regrets. I thought about the relationship I didn't have with my parents and how uncomfortable it is for me to even call them. I thought about how I would regret not calling them if they passed away. I also thought a lot about my firstborn son that I gave up all those years ago. I prayed to God that He would forgive me before I leave this earth. I am grateful that God was patient with me and allowed me to grow as a person and even though all these thoughts and memories were haunting, they were necessary to bring me to the next level. I began to realize how wretched I had behaved since moving to Hawaii—my lousy attitude and my lack of gratitude. Here I was living in one of the most beautiful places on earth, and for the past three years, I griped and complained and was ungrateful. Now I was alone and I missed my daughter and grandkids. God was doing a work in my life, and He had me held at attention up on the mountain. It was just what I needed. I struggled with thoughts of doubt about my salvation. How could I be saved if I allowed things to irritate me so much and get on my nerves? The Bible says if we don't have love, we have nothing. He was moving me forward to look inward and see what needed changing.

Chapter 12
Learning to be Grateful

Daveed had moved off the property shortly before Dawn started dating Ravyn. One Saturday afternoon he came up to pick up some of his stuff. I was relaxing and didn't go down to see him while he was getting his stuff together. He left and the next day Mark tells me he had an asthma attack later Saturday night and had passed out and hit a fence. He was in the hospital on life support, and it wasn't looking good. I was devastated that I hadn't taken the time to go down and talk with him before he left that day. I prayed and asked God to please spare his life. I went to the hospital to see him, and it was heartbreaking to see him lying in the bed with breathing tubes. I held his hand and prayed with him. I told him to forgive those who hurt him and I told him to accept Christ. I believe he heard me because people who are in comas say they could hear what was going on.

He passed away that Wednesday, and it was a real blow to

my son and our family. He was young. He had severe asthma and had taken really good care of himself because he knew it could be deadly. Not having him at Dawn's wedding was sad; he sure was missed. His mother and sister came to the island to take care of all the formalities. I was blessed to meet his mom and tried to bring her comfort. It was another wakeup call at how fast things can happen and how precious life is. It just made me appreciate my family even more. It was a blessing that Dawn had Ravyn to help her through the loss because she had become good friends with Daveed.

Several months later, we all went on a camping trip to Kona. It's the dry side of the island. When we got back from the trip, Dawn messaged me and told me my good friend Lisa had posted on Facebook that she had been diagnosed with lung cancer. Lisa and Tammy were sisters, and I had lost Tammy years before like I mentioned. I immediately messaged Lisa and let her know I would be here for her through this difficult time. I had experience with it since Dawn had survived. We sent voice messages back and forth every day, sometimes all day long. I was no longer feeling as lonely now that I had her to talk to. I did my best to reassure her that she could beat this. We prayed together and reminisced about the past. We talked about everything under the sun. We talked about God a lot and our kids. She had explained to me how she came to realize that she needed to get scanned. She had been really sick for six months. She was coughing and couldn't seem to get better. Beth Chapman from *Dog the Bounty Hunter* had just passed away, and she was watching an episode where Beth was saying if you have a cold you can't get over or a constant tickle in your throat, don't hesitate to go get a scan. Lisa said when she heard that it hit her like a ton of bricks. She went and got the scan and sure enough she had lung cancer. She was a heavy smoker, and her smoking had increased since the overdose death of her son several years earlier. I pleaded with her to quit, and her stress levels were so high due to many family situations that she just couldn't completely put them down. She had planned on getting surgery and coming out to Hawaii so I could nurse her back to health. We had plans for me to take her around the island and show her how beautiful it was here. Six weeks after she was diagnosed, her husband Louie was talking to her in the kitchen when the side of his mouth began to droop. We were messaging back and forth when this was happening. She sends me a message and says she insisted he go to urgent care right away because she thought he was having a stroke. She sends me a voice message a little while later saying they sent him to the hospital for head scans. It wasn't long after that she sent me a desperate message screaming that Louie has multiple tumors on his brain, and it looks like cancer.

I couldn't believe what I was hearing. She was a complete mess and all I could do was pray. When it was all said and done, he was also diagnosed with the same lung cancer as Lisa. It had spread to his brain and bones. It was a nightmare and from there everything changed. Lisa put her own care on the back burner and had to take care of Louie. She had tried some alternative treatments because she was dead set against chemo. Louie had radiation, and it took a terrible toll on him. He was declining rapidly. I did my best to give her support and tried to speak life over both of them. Unfortunately, she watched as this cruel disease took her husband away from her. She had so much faith, but sadly he just couldn't beat it and he passed away. She had been getting fluid drained from her lungs every week it seemed like. Her youngest daughter was pregnant with her grand baby. She tried to do immunotherapy, but she had waited too long. Her trips to the hospital became more frequent and our talks became less. I was devastated when I got the news from her friend that she was not likely to be leaving the hospital. I tried to call her one last time, but she didn't want to talk. Her daughter gave birth to a baby girl the night before Lisa passed away.

I hadn't felt this kind of pain in a long time. I cried for three days, and then the peace and comfort of Christ just took over. I miss her terribly, and it was hard for me not to come home and listen to all her messages she would leave me every day. Cancer took them both in a year's time. I'll never understand why, but it was another wake up call for me to appreciate what and who I have in my life. Any moment things can change. In the midst of everything happening with Lisa, Covid reared its ugly head. I knew it was coming because in the beginning of the year, I was seeing videos from China on YouTube. I told Dawn she might want to cancel Ava's upcoming heart appointment on Oahu because her immune system is compromised. I really wasn't worried about the lock down and had no fear of getting sick. My only real concern was for Ava. It seemed as if every time she went to Honolulu for medical issues, she always got sick a few days later. She needed to get a stent put in heart sooner than later due to the fact her little heart was working overtime. We could all feel it when she laid next to us. The area over her top lip was turning blue as well so that was another indicator that it needed to be done. Medical care on these islands are sub-par. We missed her wonderful cardiologist from Virginia. He was a Christian, and Dawn had his cell number in case anything happened or she had questions. The doctor she now sees doesn't even read her chart half the time and seems like he never knows what is going on with Ava. One of the downsides of living in Hawaii is poor medical care. She recently had the procedure done and should be good for a while. I don't want to think about her having another open-heart surgery. We are believing God to completely heal her. She is absolutely beautiful and very loving. My life has been so much more blessed with that little girl in it. I was upset when Dawn was pregnant, but I of all people should know that all children are a precious gift from God.

The best thing that ever happened to me beside Jesus is my children and my grandchildren. I'm 100% pro-life. I don't think there is any reason to kill a baby in the womb and that includes rape or incest. I was young and lacked life skills when I had my kids, but God knows the beginning from the end. There is always a way to make it work one way or another. If you feel like you can't keep the baby, then put it up for adoption. I wholeheartedly believe that abortion destroys more than just the life of the child. It takes a terrible toll on the mothers. The guilt and shame will haunt them for years. God is a merciful Father, and if women repent for having the abortion, then He is faithful to forgive.

My life's journey has been one with many twists and turns, but through it all I learned that I am a fighter. Even when I wasn't seeking him, God was with me all the time. I enjoy and love my family. There has been a lot of heartache and heartbreak, but God has also helped to restore what was once broken. I believe that He is still working on our family, and I'm trusting that one day that call from my father will come. God is a healer, and I'm ready for all that He has for me. I have been tested and tried throughout my whole life, so I know I can survive anything that comes my way as long as I have the Lord on my side.

May God continue to bless you on your life's journey as

well. If anything shared within the pages of this book bears witness with you and your lifestyle, know that God can turn it around. Ask the Holy Spirit to come live in your heart and direct your steps. Know that as you enter a relationship with Jesus, He will intercede on your behalf. Trust that the Father only wants good for you, but as you move closer to Him, the enemy's grip will intensify, but know as the scriptures say, "Greater is he that is in me, then he that is in the world." What this means is the Holy Spirit lives inside of you and the enemy is of this world. The power of the Holy Spirit is greater and more precious than anything this world can offer you. Be blessed and God be with you.

www.ingramcontent.com/pod-product-compliance
Lightning Source LLC
Chambersburg PA
CBHW071207160426
43196CB00011B/2215